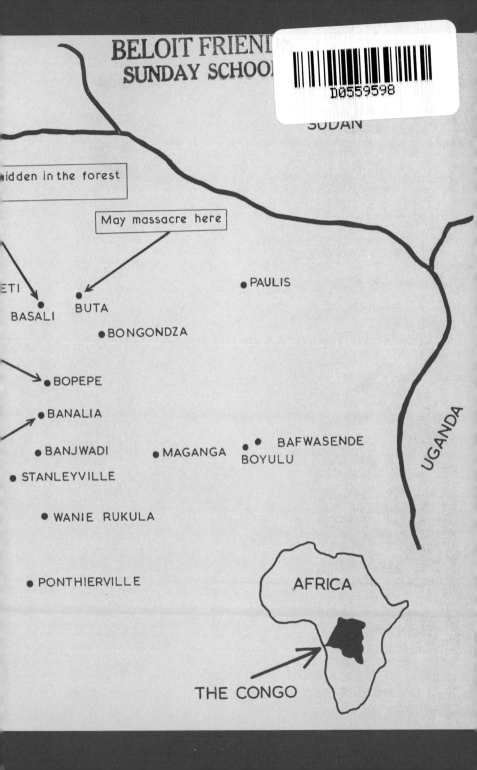

CAPTIVE OF THE SIMBAS

CAPTIVE OF
THE SIMBAS

MARGARET HAYES

HARPER & ROW, PUBLISHERS

NEW YORK AND EVANSTON

Photographs on the following pages of the picture section have been used through the courtesy of the Unevangelised Fields Mission: page 2 (upper); page 3 (lower); page 5 (lower); page 7; and page 8.

Captive of the Simbas was published in England under the title
Missing—Believed Killed.

LIBRARY OF CONGRESS CATALOG CARD NUMBER: 66-20777

Missionary Book for 1968 - 1969.

Vercia Cox Circle Readers.

Freda Gisberger

DEDICATED TO ALL MY MANY
CONGOLESE BROTHERS AND SISTERS

Ethel F. Naylor

Georgeanny Townsend.

Elsie Hooper

"The struggle for the soul of Africa must involve Missions and missionaries, for much that has come to the needy continent came from the hands of missionaries. So often in human history the missionary pioneer has made a road over which much good and evil has travelled, but that is the price for road making. The white and coloured peoples are locked in conflict over the vast continent of Africa, but of one thing we may be sure. While Africa has such dedicated people as Margaret Hayes, there will be a helpful, healing ministry that may point Africans to live above the clash of politics, racial hatred and the greed for the Western way of life, for it is forever true that 'the blood of the martyrs is the seed of the church'."

LEONARD F. HARRIS
General Secretary,
Unevangelised Fields Mission

Foreword

"It's fantastic — she gave herself up, what a woman! What faith! I don't know what I would do, I admit I haven't got a faith."

We were at London Airport waiting for the plane that was to bring Margaret home. There was an electrifying sense of excitement and controlled impatience. We were by no means a small group; as well as relations, friends and mission representatives, newspaper and magazine reporters and television cameramen were there. Margaret Hayes was a V.I.P. and her name larger than life because she embodied the courage, love and devotion of her missionary colleagues who had been massacred in the Congo uprising. While we waited, a reporter spoke to me in the words I have quoted above.

He was there because Margaret was news; as another reporter said quite ruthlessly, "This is a good line." But he recognised something special about this piece of news. He was conscious of a quality in Margaret that defied ordinary explanation. Rightly he attributed it to her faith and admitted sadly that he would not know what to do in a similar crisis: "I haven't got a faith." But Margaret has a faith and because of this she was sustained throughout her terrifying experiences.

At the time when hopes for her safety were fading, the *Daily Sketch* devoted its leading article to her. Referring to the three letters which were smuggled out of Congo during her captivity, it numbered her with the truly great. It linked her name with that of Captain Scott of the Antarctic, and with Anne Frank, a young Jewess who died at the hands of the Nazis. The paper said, "Through the darkness of savagery and hatred in the

Congo, there shines one ray of light. That ray is the faith of Margaret Hayes."

I have been impressed in reading Hebrews, chapter 11, that the experiences of the people of faith were not identical. Some had faith to die triumphantly, others faith to be delivered. In both cases their faith was honoured. As I write, I pause to thank God for the illustrious number of Congo missionaries who were given faith to lay down their lives, and to overcome by the blood of the Lamb and by the word of their testimony.

Margaret has miraculously survived. Twice given up for dead, she was protected, upheld and delivered to the praise and glory of God and to the overwhelming gratitude of her loved ones and many friends. Margaret takes her place among the noble company, "Who through faith stopped the mouths of lions . . . escaped the edge of the sword."

God has written for ever in her memory a record of His faithful and tender dealings with her. Now she shares her experiences with us in this book that she has written. I am sure that it will be eagerly read by a wide and varied company. The book is thrilling, moving, challenging and humbling. To read it seriously is a spiritual exercise. One newspaper article referring to her letters said, "Margaret Hayes spent fifteen years of her life as a down to earth London nurse. Fine words do not fit her." With the last sentence I cannot agree. Fine words do suit Margaret; she has a deceptively simple style that flows along, carrying her readers forward with increasing interest. Margaret has not read the classics in vain; some of her favourites she lost at Bopepe.

This book is a poignant account of a woman's love for the Lord and for the Congolese whose servant, for Christ's sake she is. As Margaret's Pastor and one whose privilege it was to visit Congo in 1963, I feel greatly honoured to write this foreword.

May the book be used beyond imagining to the blessing of

the many people who read it. The story is more than fantastic, it is phenomenal.

"Blessed be the Lord God, the God of Israel, Who only doeth wondrous things. And blessed be His glorious name for ever and ever; Amen and Amen." Psalm 72: 18–19.

PAUL TUCKER
East London Baptist Tabernacle

Preface

IT was whilst I was a prisoner that the idea came to me to write this book, and since our dramatic rescue from the Congolese rebels, there has been ample time for so doing.

My diary was destroyed, which I began whilst with the rebels, so not all minor events are in chronological order.

Towards the end of writing the book, my Bible and *Daily Light* were found in the forest and they were sent on to me. In these I had kept my prison diary and events up to December 1964, therefore the incidents recorded for these two months are correct for both time and date.

My grateful thanks are due to Mr. Geoffrey Bull for permission to quote from his book *God Holds the Key*.

This book would never have been finished on time had it not been for the gallant effort of my sister, Mrs. Eileen Sodeau, and my sister-in-law, Mrs. Ann Hayes, who had to wade through pages of my poor handwriting. Also a tremendous word of praise for Miss Joyce Conridge who so patiently typed and retyped the entire manuscript in spite of being otherwise fully employed.

To Mr. David Truby, who read, advised, and guided me through all the technicalities of writing a book, a special word of thanks. To the Rev. Paul Tucker, my Pastor, who has lent photographs, as all mine were destroyed in Congo, and who has graciously consented to write the foreword, my grateful thanks.

Lastly, a word of thanks to all who have stood behind me in this venture in prayer.

If this book causes the reader to pause and think and praise the Lord Jesus Christ, it will have been worthwhile.

M. H.

Contents

Picture section follows page 96

I

Revolution Simba!

THE village of Bopepe was very much like other Congolese villages, an untidy collection of mud-walled houses with leaf-roofs, but at one end it was obvious that it was more than just an ordinary village. It boasted a brick church (all bricks made by the villagers), a six-roomed, mud and cement school, three houses built similarly; all these buildings had metal roofs. A little further on, behind the school, one could see the now transformed football field, housing the dispensary buildings, simply made with mud and leaves. Bopepe was situated in the middle of Congo's vast forest land and about ninety-five miles from the provincial capital, the city of Stanleyville, to which there was easy access if one had the transport, as the main highway to Stanleyville ran alongside the village.

July 1964 was a busy month for us at Bopepe, for in addition to our usual programme we had to prepare for a conference of our church leaders; certainly none of us envisaged, except Pastor Asani, the far-seeing leading pastor of the Unevangelized Fields Mission, and President of the Congo Protestant Council, that our corner of Congo would be plunged into a very bloody revolution within three weeks. Plans were made for various aspects of the mission's work, some of them for the immediate future and some for the more distant days ahead. Pastor Asani, the quietly spoken, tall, lanky and bespectacled man, who together with his identical but noisier twin brother, Pastor Bo Martin, lived at Bopepe, had a premonition of a terrible time coming; he had often talked to us about the unrest in the Congo, and several times had said that a time was approaching in which we would witness terrible things and much bloodshed. In fact he did not really want the conference to be held at all, as it would mean a large number of people being together in a small area.

However, the permits all came through in time, the local chief even promised us a whole animal from his cattle – though he changed his mind later, and eventually both Congolese and white folk came to Bopepe from every station. It was a wonderful time of fellowship and making new friends. Our little house was packed, in fact I think most Bopepe houses were bursting at the seams!

Looking back I see it as a very precious time spent with others of like faith. It was to be the last time we would all meet in that way again, and for some it was the last conference.

We were equipped with a transceiver, that is a radio on which we contacted our other stations on a fixed wave length at a pre-arranged time each day. It was amusing to see all our menfolk, who appeared to be so terribly independent when away from their wives, crowd into our little office in order to speak and listen to them on their respective stations, and to see the gleam of satisfaction on their faces when all was reported well.

The week culminated in a very challenging service, our preacher being the Rev. Bob McAllister, a heavyweight Irishman, who could have his congregation rocking with laughter one minute and weeping the next. He preached to us on "If it be possible let this cup pass from me, nevertheless not as I will, but as thou wilt". I do not think any of us came away from that service unmoved by the stirring message we had heard. How many times was I to pray that prayer in future days!

The folks left and went their various ways, some on vacation, others back to their stations to carry on the work of bringing the Gospel to those still in darkness.

Our stores were depleted and a trip to Stanleyville, ninety-five miles away, was imperative in the very near future. Owing

16

to the pressure of work over the previous two years I was very tired and very reluctantly agreed with Mary Baker, my missionary co-worker at Bopepe, that I must get away for a rest. It was decided I should leave on August 1st and go to Banjwadi, a large U.F.M. station, where they had a flourishing medical work, an overflowing primary school, and a newly created Seminary for the training of Congolese pastors. This station was only forty miles from Stanleyville. I was to be away for a month and at the same time I could go into town as occasion permitted and shop. Mary would come down during the third week, pick up a new Volkswagen Camionette, which was due from Belgium in August, and also collect the shopping and me, and we would return to Bopepe on August 30th.

We were alarmingly short of nurses at that time, not that we ever have too many! Most of us were having to close down our dispensaries in order to have a vacation, because there was no one to relieve us. Often I thought of the hundreds of Christian nurses at home, and wished that some would come out and help us; it is such a rich, satisfying ministry.

I felt mean leaving the folks for a whole month. However, August 1st dawned, and I tied up the ends of work, left Mary with a well-equipped first aid box, and lots of instructions on how to give out various pills, and anyway, we would be in radio contact every day in case anything alarming happened.

The opportunity to have a lift in a car had fallen through, and it was decided I should go to Banjwadi by autobus. It was a boneshaker if ever there was one; the driver, who was well known to us, thought he was a jet pilot judging by the way he drove! The bus, as usual, was late, and I decided that if it was not through by 5.30 p.m. the Lord obviously did not mean me to go. He came at 5.25. Practically the entire village came to see me off. Congo roads are not noted for their even surfaces, and the further one penetrates into the interior the worse they become, with potholes several feet wide, or wash-board surfaces, so for the bus to travel the fifteen miles in twenty minutes was exceptionally fast, especially in view of the fact that not only was the bus full, but it also carried a long trailer too!

We almost reached the town of Banalia – a small town which boasted a post-office, administrator's post, a government hospital, and also two large catholic schools, one for boys and one for girls – but were separated from it by a wide river called the Aruwimi, which had to be crossed by a ferry.

There were other trucks there when we arrived and the ferry took them over and then refused to come back for us. They said it was 6.30 and work was through for the day. My incredulity gave place to resignation, and finding two men who were willing to take me in their canoe, I made my way to the Government doctor's house on the other side of the river. He was a middle-aged Frenchman, serving with the World Health Organisation, and we had known him for just over a year and often exchanged visits with him and his wife and children. He was very hospitable and housed me that night. The nine o'clock news from France did not mention Congo at all, but the B.B.C. at ten o'clock told of various trouble spots which were springing up throughout the North-East Province. We talked about the possibility of anything coming our way, but left the question very much open to speculation.

Sunday morning the bus duly crossed on the ferry and once more I was on my way. The driver sang excerpts from the Requiem Mass all the way! He had a beautiful tenor voice but it was hardly a comforting theme song to which to listen as the bus and trailer bounded along at an incredibly hair-raising speed. As it was impossible to hear anyone speak above the din of the rattles of the bus and the vocal efforts of the driver, I was more than glad when we arrived at our destination at midday. A large number of my fellow travellers were young men, well dressed, and most were carrying briefcases. I have often wondered what happened to them subsequently, as they were all bound for Stanleyville.

Arriving at Banjwadi, I very guiltily made my way past the church which was not only packed inside but had a crowd outside. I felt like a pagan who had suddenly found herself in the midst of a Christian mission, and very uncomfortable was the feeling, though I vindicated my nagging conscience by saying that in the normal course of events I should have arrived the day before and therefore would have been in church instead of just arriving hot and sticky and very dusty on a Sunday morning.

It was a joy to meet up again with our beloved Dr. Ian Sharpe, a young and very gifted doctor from England, who endeared himself to all and sundry by his winning personality. His wife, Audrey, was with him. She was a nurse, also from England; she had been ill several times and it was a real joy to see how well she looked. With them were also their three tow-headed children, Jillian, aged eight years, Alison, aged seven, and Andrew (Andy), aged four. All three spoke Lingala fluently, and Andy spoke also some French and an unwritten tribal language called Kibua. Also with the doctor and his family was another co-worker, Miss Ruby Gray, a nurse from Ireland, in her first term. These all came from one of our stations called Bongondza, which had a hospital and school, and was approximately eighty miles further north of the village of Bopepe. There was a new missionary family to meet – the Davis's: "Chuck" Davis and his wife Muriel and their two children from the United States. They had been in Congo three months and had spent just one week at Banjwadi where Chuck was going to teach in the Seminary.

All the usual residents of Banjwadi had gone on vacation, leaving two newly-arrived from furlough. David Grant and his wife Sonia were from Canada, and had been back in Congo exactly one month. David was one of those fellows who could turn his hand to almost anything, and was always much in demand by everybody; from fixing a lock on a door to con-structing a water-tank to supply the entire station, nothing was too trivial or too hard for his attention. His wifeSonia, a nurse of high competence, equalled him in her work in the dispensary and maternity. Their own house was not yet free, so they were living in the house of the Seminary Director, Rev. Marshall Southard, who was in Leopoldville attending a conference; his wife Thelma and young five-year-old Larry were, we hoped, en route back to Banjwadi after a vacation in Kenya. They were due in on August 5th. The Muchmore family, Mum and Dad and two sons, had just gone home to America on furlough the previous Friday, and the John Artons from England were away up country; they had gone to meet their only daughter Heather, who was coming out for her summer vacation. The Morris family, with one very young son, were home in England on a month's vacation paid for by the Congolese Government.

This was the situation locally when I arrived on what seemed to us a perfectly normal Sunday morning, when war was far from our minds, though in fact it had already involved two of our stations.

The Grants stretched the already large table, and somehow in the evening, we all sat round it— the five Sharpes, four Davis's, two Grants, Ruby Gray, and myself. There were four nationalities represented; American, Canadian, English and Irish.

Later that evening we met for a service, Ian Sharpe played the little organ, and Chuck Davis gave us the Word. It seemed a perfectly normal, happy Congo Sunday, but strangely enough it was the last normal one we were to experience. The following morning Dr. Sharpe and family, and Ruby Gray, left for Bongondza. Arrangements were made to follow their progress over the radio; we expected them to be at Bopepe by midday.

Midday came, and when we tuned in to our Headquarters in Stanleyville, it was to hear our Field Secretary, Al Larson, say that our small station of Wanie Rukula, comprising a dispensary and primary school, situated right on the equator itself, and lying approximately forty miles south east of Stanleyville, had been off the air since Saturday, and they were very anxious as news of rebel advances in that area was disturbing. It was decided that they would call back all Stations at 4 p.m. In the meantime we would pray. At four o'clock there was still no news, and reports coming in to Stanleyville were not very reassuring. We were told to have a bag packed in case of sudden emergency, and in case we had to be evacuated out of the area.

That night as we met for prayers before going to bed, David read from *Daily Light* (August 3rd evening): "Fear none of these things which thou shalt suffer. Be thou faithful unto death . . ." It was with very heavy hearts that we separated, though not to sleep. We thought and prayed for the folks at Wanie Rukula – the Gesheidles, Volka and Else from Germany; they were in their first term, and due to vacations were alone on the station. We thought of all our Congolese friends there and wondered . . .

By next morning, the Congolese were standing in little worried groups outside the house. The B.B.C. had announced rapid advances being made in all areas around Stanleyville; we could hardly wait for midday. There was still no news from Wanie Rukula, and shooting was reported to be very near Stanleyville, approximately ten miles from the city. Our field secretary, Al Larson, said that those who wished to leave the country were to do so immediately; those who were near to Stanleyville were to come in, as planes were at the disposal of evacuees, the women and children to go first. Al said that he himself would not leave the country whilst there was one of us still here, unless he were forced to leave.

Quite honestly, I do not know what we thought would happen, but we remembered the 1960 evacuation, and I guess most of us had felt badly enough about that. We decided to stay and carry on our work. This was the decision of every station. Mary Baker was alone at Bopepe, but thinking it would be a similar situation to 1960, when there was much panic but little subsequent action, we were not too worried at that stage.

It was decided we should all call Headquarters on the radio hourly, on the hour. It is surprising how quickly an hour goes when one is busy; it seemed as though we had hardly put down the microphone when it was time to listen in again. By now, little groups of Congolese would be either in the sitting-room, or outside the windows, waiting for us to interpret the latest bulletin. It was far from encouraging. Curfew in Stanleyville from 3.30 p.m. to 7 a.m. All roads closed. Advance of the rebels around Stanleyville, the airport captured; then the national radio was off the air, only to come back again, a day later, in rebel hands.

We had felt right from the first that we should lay aside all unnecessary work and concentrate on prayer, so we would meet and pray five or six times a day. These were times of great encouragement to us, and as we read the Word of God, it brought new peace to our troubled thoughts.

Al Larson then gave the order that nobody was to leave their stations, as the National Army was in flight and the rebels were right on their heels. Knowing how we felt at Banjwadi, and we were seven in number, I began to wonder about Mary Baker alone there at Bopepe. The whole thing had become a nightmare, and I did not think it fair to stay on at Banjwadi, whilst Mary was alone. Permission was granted for me to go if safe transport could be guaranteed.

By now, various folk were stranded. Thelma and Larry Southard were at Boyulu, our furthest north-eastern station where we had a large medical and education program. They were about two hundred miles from Stanleyville itself, and would have had to go through the city in order to reach Banjwadi, their home station. Hector McMillan, Canadian born, and, like David Grant, able to turn his hand to practically anything, was stranded with two of his six sons at Boyulu, while his wife and the four other children were in Stanleyville.

Their station was Bongondza, where Dr. and Mrs. Sharpe and Ruby Gray also worked. The Artons, now with the addition of their sixteen-year-old daughter, were also caught there en route to Banjwadi.

Miss Jean Sweet, an English teacher in her first term, was spending her long vacation from her station at Boyulu, helping with the young people's vacation Bible School. Also stranded there was our only Australian worker, Miss Laurel McCullum, who was en route back to her own station of Wanie Rukula, to take up her work again amongst the children of the area.

There were the normal staff complement at Boyulu. Miss Olive McCarten, an English teacher, was going to spend the vacation with Jean Sweet, working amongst the young people. Veteran missionary Miss Louie Rimmer, also from England, was there, coping quite ably with her work amongst the women and girls of the school and outlying area. Station leaders Chester and Dolena Burk from Canada had not left the station, though they too were in need of a rest after a hard term in school for Dolena, and supervising the work generally and teaching in the local Bible School for Chester.

Days went by; still no news from Wanie Rukula, and Al Larson's Stanleyville news was not very encouraging. A cablegram was sent out to the U.S.A. and London Headquarters, via radio to the Africa Inland Mission radio station who were at that time unaffected by all this as they were further north. They received the answer and radioed it back to us. We were very grateful to A.I.M. for their help in this matter. Eventually the time came when Al Larson advised the A.I.M. to get out whilst they could, as this rebel movement was definitely anti-American, and most of their missionaries were Americans. They were all able to get away without loss of life.

In order to keep a certain amount of secrecy about our conversations on the air, the rebel army were called "Robert" and the National Army "Louis". During those early days the rebels were an unknown quantity to us, and we had the usual human tendency to fear the unknown. I can remember the day when Al Larson had told us that if he went off the air suddenly it was because the rebels were in the house or grounds, but we were to stay tuned in, and yet to maintain radio silence amongst other stations. Then right in the middle of a sentence, he suddenly said "Robert has arrived," and a weighty silence fell – we held our breath at Banjwadi, visualising all sorts of things happening to our folks there, and praying at the same time for all we were worth.

Strange the various memories that come crowding back; the preciousness of the Word of God, how it seemed that every reading was geared to the specific needs of the moment. Even the devotional readings from F. B. Meyer and Spurgeon, which David would read to us after a meal, were pertinent to the times in which we found ourselves, yet Spurgeon had lived one hundred years before! And as for that little book *Daily Light*, I wonder if others have ever noticed how much there is in it about trouble and the way the Lord will undertake for us. Best of all, of course, were our regular Bible readings; we all had different ways of Bible Study and were studying different portions, yet when we compared notes and thoughts, it was amazing how they all seemed to coincide somehow.

One day on the radio we had failed to get a response from Mary Baker at Bopepe, and we carried on, when suddenly we heard Mary calling us and asking us to call her in as she had ten Simbas (Simba is the Swahili word for lion) or rebels in the office with her and they wanted to know why Mary had the radio. Ian Sharpe and Hector McMillan both spoke to the Simbas, who were finally convinced that it was not a broadcast to America; but all the same they said they would have to take the set. After this, one by one the stations went off the air; we heard a call from Leopoldville, from Marshall Southard, and on one occasion were able to answer, but the next day we had promised the Simbas that we would not speak to Leopoldville, and it was awful hearing them call and not daring to answer.

All these radio broadcasts could be picked up on an ordinary radio. After almost three weeks, they came one evening and took the Banjwadi radio too.

Our first encounter with the Simbas was our second weekend; we were by this time still on the air and were later able to warn Mary Baker that they were on their way to her. A Land Rover pulled in and stopped outside our home; out jumped Dr. John Saether of the Norwegian Baptist Mission. We had studied together in Antwerp, and lived in the same house whilst there. He had three other N.B.M. missionaries with him and two fierce-looking Simbas. The latter would not enter the house, so we studied them from the shelter of the doorway. They looked perfectly ordinary people except that they would not smile, only scowl; they were fully clothed (some later were half naked), they also had the additional fur pieces on their wrists, their charms against death, fur on their hats, and they carried rifles. It is our custom to offer hospitality to all travellers, so we asked them if they would like some coffee or tea. One refused to answer or even turn round – we found out later he was a local boy and was probably a little ashamed. The other agreed to a cup of coffee if "Bwana made it" – so dear, obliging David made it. I took it out to him. By this time a crowd had gathered, probably as apprehensive as curious. We were all astonished when the men curtly ordered me to put the cup and saucer on the ground. Having been trained in the school of "obey first, and question later", I promptly obeyed, placing a beautiful decorative bone china cup and saucer on the muddy ground. He then picked it up and drank the coffee, and returned the cup to the ground, from where I later recovered it. In those days they were not allowed to eat anything made by a woman, nor could they receive anything from a woman. This idea persisted right up to the end of November. Everything had to be put down on the ground or a table, in order that they could pick it up without contact in any way.

Dr. Saether told us they had "baptised" his car, in order to make it invulnerable to bullets if ambushed on the road. It must have been a peculiar sensation for Baptists to watch the "baptism" of their car by Simbas! We asked the doctor if he would take me through with him to Bopepe, as he was going to stay there overnight, but there was not room, so I had to content myself with just a hurried note to Mary.

The National Army were hopelessly outnumbered in Stanleyville, and many who were captured were brutally murdered, so in a way we could hardly blame those still alive for getting out whilst they could. They would come into Banjwadi, tired, hungry and desperate, we would give them something to eat, such as bananas, etc., or gasoline for their cars, and wave them off. Most of them had their wives and children with them. They knew what their end would be if caught by the rebels.

One day we had a note from the local Roman Catholic Priest, asking what news there was on our radio, and asking us to get help for a little white family about twenty miles away, who were stranded on their plantation, *but they asked too late.*

The priests also very kindly sent us fresh vegetables and salad from their gardens, as they knew we usually bought from town, and would be short now.

Another time the question arose regarding buying party political cards, we heard that the young people's movement, (*jeunesse*) was in the area, forcing people to buy the card. Our field director advised us against buying such a card, unless life was threatened, but though we were later approached about buying them at Bopepe, and warned about the consequences if we did not, we were not forced to submit. The local population had to have them, and later it spelt virtual death to any who did not possess one, or who belonged to a different party.

Another day we noticed that the village folk were in a state of excitement and were walking about with bunches of flowers, and we were told that the "Big Man" (*Mutu Mukubwa*) was coming down and would pass by us en route to Banalia and Buta. So typical of the rebels, he was four days late! We heard

26

his approach by rifles being fired into the air, every mile or so. The village folk asked if we would go down the road to meet him, but we decided against, on the grounds that we were foreigners, and he was not really our "Big Man"; but if he came in we would give him a cup of tea. He stopped at the station entrance, and gave the usual party political talk: "The people for the people, no more tribes, soon all will be equal", etc. etc. They were also told to protect and help the white people.

By this time the Simbas had taken cars and trucks from most of our stations; not taken, just "borrowed for the duration", and with a duly signed receipt in triplicate in order to get them back later ...

It is not surprising that during this first month, food, though necessary, was not enjoyed as before; and Sonia Grant is a wonderful cook, yet we just could not find an appetite. It helped even less when if we were at the table a truck of Simbas would drive in. Somehow it seemed as though our stomachs just contracted down.

One night, as we were praying together, we heard somebody coughing outside the door. It proved to be two or three men from the village who had come to tell us to flee across the river as the *jeunesse* were on their way, and we would be in for trouble. I will always remember Sonia Grant serenely saying, "We will not run away, if we have to die, then we'll die here", and the baffled look on the faces of the men. About half an hour later, another man came; evidently he had been urged to come by the others who were so afraid for us, and to him the same answer was given. We did not feel particularly brave, but happily our faith in the Lord does not depend on our feelings! We prayed together and went to bed. In comparing notes in the morning, we were amused to find out that we had all only half undressed, so that we could be up in a minute if the rebels came, and also, that none of us had slept, we had strained our ears all night to listen for people who did not come! We laughed about it in the morning, but we all felt nonetheless ashamed of the fear we had in our hearts. "Perfect love casts out fear" – how much our love to the Lord needs perfecting . . .

A lovely respite from the constant demands of the rebels was the day a young Simba asked for a Bible. We told him to come back the next day for it, as it had to be brought out from the stores, and we did not particularly want the Simbas inspecting everything on the station. The next morning, sure enough he was back, and as Sonia walked out of the house with the Bible in her hand, to see the look of joy in the face of the Simba was indeed beautiful; he was in fact so overjoyed, he took it directly from Sonia's hand, instead of the customary putting it on the ground. How our prayers followed both the boy and the Book!

One quiet Saturday afternoon, our peace was shattered by the arrival of a car, and the officer in charge asked David about the nationalities of the white people. Only the Davis's were American, and I felt proud of Chuck, though I am very much British, for when the officer asked him his nationality, he almost stood to attention and said loudly and clearly with obvious pride in his country, "I am an American," and then showed his papers. The officer said he had to take him and his family to Stanleyville as the American Consul had asked for them to go to the Consulate; he showed us a paper on which were the names of several of our American missionaries, headed by Al Larson and family, with their addresses.

How easily we were fooled, though there was nothing we could do; they only knew one word – obey or else. Sonia and David took the officer into the house for a cup of coffee, and I went down to the Davis's house. The two children were asleep, it was siesta time. Very hurriedly they packed the last-minute things into a case, left the dog and house to us, and were in the car.

As the officer entered the car, they made the usual Simba greeting, "*Simba! Simba! Simba! Mayi! Mayi! Lumumba Mayi!*"

... and then the officer asked if there was any *"mateka"*. The answer was yes. We did not know what that meant then.

As the car drove off, we were very apprehensive, more so when the Africans who had been standing around explained to us the meaning of *mateka*. It is a Swahili and Lingala word meaning "butter" and the Simbas used it for "death", for if they found an African able to afford butter, it was immediately assumed he was obtaining money illegally, and therefore must die, so for them the word was synonymous with death. We prayed and prayed, yet the awful presentiment of danger did not leave us. The officer had promised that they would return next day, but we were beginning to find out what good liars they were. The Davis's had a nightmare journey to town; remember they had two children with them, a boy of four years, and a wee girl of eighteen months. They were made to witness a man shot down, rifles pointing at them in the car, and finally when they arrived, not at the Consulate, but on the outskirts of the city at the Airport Hotel, they were told to get out of the car, helped by rifle butts, and made to enter the men's toilet. There they found to everybody's mutual amazement, the American Consul and four of his staff. After a little while they were taken outside and lined up against a wall as though to be shot. Muriel prayed that they would all die together. However, the Simbas changed their minds and decided to let Muriel and the children go, and keep Chuck and the other men imprisoned.

A car was produced to take Muriel to the military camp, but happily, in the Lord's providential care, there was not enough gas in the car. In the centre of the town lived our two most senior missionaries, Mr. and Mrs. Jenkinson (known affectionately by black and white alike as Kinso and Ma Kinso). They were in charge of a large literature store called LECO. Muriel quickly remembered this, and that it was in the centre of the town, opposite the prison. She prevailed upon the chauffeur to go there, and just as dusk was falling they arrived. Chuck was later moved to the general prison and cruelly beaten together with the other men, and made to undergo great privations. Eventually he was released after seventeen days, though the other men were imprisoned until November 24th.

Meanwhile, ninety miles north of Stanleyville, and eighteen miles from Banalia, in a small village called Bodela which had only just newly acquired missionaries to live and work amongst them, was the Parry family. Dennis Parry, an English evangelist, was in church taking the afternoon meeting. His wife Nora, a nurse from England, who looked so frail, and yet was beginning to build up a medical work in the area, was at home in the house with their two young children, teaching them, as there was not a Sunday School for them to attend, and they were both home from school for the summer vacation. A car with six Simbas pulled up outside and the men went into the house. They verbally abused Nora, and then hit her, knocking her across the room and losing her spectacles at the same time. The children were afraid, though Andrew, almost eleven years old, did not show it; but Grace, just eight, was very upset. They next went and found Dennis, pulled him out of the church and abused him. They demanded the jeep. Dennis explained that the battery was dead and therefore the car would not go, there was also some other fault. They surrounded him and made him repair it, saying they would return for it in two hours. Leaving two Simbas to guard him, they went off, returning four hours later, very drunk. Dennis finally proved his point, but they said he had deliberately put the car out of action so that they could not have it; then they locked the car and went off with the keys.

At Bongondza, one hundred and twenty miles from Stanleyville, the doctor and his family were in the house, when another car load of Simbas arrived there. They had arrested Masini Phillipe, the brave and faithful pastor of the Bongondza church and father of five children, and, calling Ian and Audrey out of the house, beat Masini unmercifully in front of them. Audrey defended Masini, and was struck across the face for her pains. The Simbas then "inspected the house", took all they wanted, including the radio set (an ordinary radio), and went away.

The Bodela group left Bodela for Banalia, and on the way the car overturned and the man who had struck Nora had an arm and a leg broken. "Vengeance is mine saith the Lord, I will repay."

At Bopepe, Mary Baker was alone, and resting during siesta time. A car with eight Simbas came and they sneaked up to the house pointing their rifles. Mary let them in. They abused her verbally for sleeping "when there was a war on", and proceeded to search the house from top to bottom. Pastor Bo Martin, twin brother of Pastor Asani, heard they had come, and demanded to be in the house with her. They said some terrible things to Mary but did not touch her. At one point they took her out on to the verandah and pointing the rifle to her cheek, asked if she wanted to die? Mary said later to me, "I wasn't afraid any more, and told them to go ahead and shoot me, as I was quite ready to die." They put the rifle down and said they admired her courage . . . Then, taking her radio, and with threats to come back and marry her, they left, after one and a half hours. The villagers, who had witnessed what had happened, were very impressed and said, "Why she looked at the gun and didn't even cry or show sign of fear . . . Truly she practises what she preaches."

Back at Banjwadi I was very burdened for Mary, and the last week in August the Lord gave the assurance that He would get me back to Bopepe. Poor David and Sonia must have been really fed up with me. It was not that I did not appreciate their hospitality, but Mary was alone, and Sonia *did* have David. The Lord gave real peace about it all, and on the following Saturday afternoon at four o'clock precisely, in came the French doctor from Banalia with a special request from the British Consul in Stanleyville to take me back to Bopepe.

"Quick, quick," he said, "I cannot wait." He did not have

to, I was prepared! At 4.5 we were on our way. How I rejoiced and praised the Lord all the way.

The journey was interesting in that we had Simba escorts, and each time we came to a village which had chickens or goats we had to stop and bargain with them for their livestock. The people were obviously terrified of the Simbas, and at times even incoherent in their answers from sheer fright. The Simbas enjoyed this new power they wielded and would add empty threats to their commands, just to see what the results would be. On several occasions the doctor pleaded with them to have pity on the poor folk.

I was shocked on first meeting the doctor; it was four weeks since I had left him in Banalia, and apparently two weeks later the Simbas came and took him to Stanleyville to work there as the chief surgeon of the area. In those two weeks he had lost eight kilos in weight (approximately sixteen pounds), and was lined and haggard and obviously under great strain.

He had an emergency operation awaiting him at Banalia, so we could not cross the ferry and again I stayed the night at Banalia, but what a difference . . . The house was full of Simbas, the house boy had two black eyes from being beaten, most of the doctor's property had been stolen, including all his sheets and blankets.

This time it was advisable to make sure that my bedroom door was locked; it did not really look too promising for a good night's rest, as Simbas were all over the house, but when I opened *Daily Light* that night, August 29th, I read "I will both lay me down in peace and sleep, for Thou Lord, only makest me dwell in safety." "Thou shalt not be afraid for the terror by night." And the last text, "I will trust and not be afraid." So I praised the Lord for His promises, and lay down and slept all night.

Morning came and the doctor greeted me with the fact that the ferry was out of order and we would therefore be returning to Banjwadi.

This did not fit in with what I thought was the Lord's plan; I felt so sure He would not have allowed me to come to within fifteen miles of Bopepe, and then let me down. He just was not that kind of God . . .

The doctor went to the hospital. I was alone, and utilised the time in prayer, stating my case quite simply and telling the Lord I knew He could get me across that river by ten o'clock in deadline with the doctor, who was in a perpetual hurry these days.

At 9.30 the doctor returned, and almost falling out of his jeep in his haste, grabbed my case and said the ferry would be able to cross right now! I will always be grateful to him for his kindness in taking me right through to Bopepe, as apparently his orders were only to Banalia. I praised the Lord all the way along. We had to pull up at one road block, but having Simbas in the car, we were allowed by unmolested.

It was 10.45 when we returned into Bopepe; all the folks were in church, but Mary came out and was so overjoyed at seeing me she burst into tears. Obviously it was hopeless to carry on the service, so the poor preacher had to hurriedly wind up the service, and have a closing hymn. As it finished, Mary asked me to pop my head into the church to greet the folks. Bless them! I was overwhelmed with their welcome. You would have thought I had been away for years instead of just one month!

2

Bopepe Days

IT was wonderful, being back where I belonged. One by one the folks came in to give their greetings, and to ask news of relatives and friends nearer to Banjwadi and Stanleyville. All six of our school teachers had been in Stanleyville at the beginning of the revolution and they, too, had experienced a very difficult time. We praised the Lord that they were all able to return to Bopepe, though it was a "near miss" for two of them. One of them, a young man called Bwanachui, father of five, was accused of being a "reactionary" simply because he knew how to read and write, and wore a white shirt and tie! He was cruelly beaten and condemned to die without even a hearing—the "people" had voted! He was imprisoned in a room with nineteen others. Later the same day, three Simbas came with machine guns, and after tying the prisoners' hands together, stood them in line in the room and shot at them. They all slumped to the floor, Bwanachui with them, but by the merciful hand of the Lord, he was not even hurt. Suddenly he heard the noise of feet running, and in came an officer who had come to find out the cause of the shooting. "What is going on here?" he demanded. The Simbas explained they had all been condemned to death by the people's court. The officer then called to see if any were still alive. Bwanachui lifted his head. They stood him up, dazed, and bloodstained from those who had fallen each side of him. *He was the only man who had survived that massacre.* On questioning, the officer could find no cause for death, and berated the Simbas for killing people who were intelligent and trained. He untied Bwanachui's hands, gave him a stick and asked him who it was who had accused him; and when he pointed them out, told him to beat them. But he had temporarily lost the use of his hands and arms from being tied, and was unable to do anything except look helplessly at his accusers. The officer then took the law into his own hands and shot them.

Poor Bwanachui arrived back at Bopepe just half an hour after his little girl of two and a half years old had died of leukaemia. Even so, his faith in the Lord never wavered whilst I was at Bopepe; and up to our arrest in November he often gave the message on Sunday mornings, and always he was inspiring and a great blessing to us.

Another teacher, our young school director, Paul Ponea, who had a new wife, was also in Stanleyville with Bwanachui; twice he was very badly beaten, and twice put on the "death-truck", and twice the Lord intervened and he was taken off at the last minute. He is a man of great potential, an excellent school director, and at the same time learning much of the things of the Spirit. He is a nephew of the twin pastors Asani and Bo Martin. Paul did not just accept all that was told him; he would think things through, and also he was maturing in the school of prayer.

At Bopepe, cut off from others, we still had my small transistor radio, and could follow the B.B.C. For days at a time there would not be any news of our part of the world.

We established a new routine, so that we could meet several times during the day to pray together. These times became increasingly precious to us as the weeks went by. Gradually we were learning to do without things we thought so necessary.

At this stage, let me tell about Mary Baker. She was a warm-hearted American from Virginia; fifty years of age though she looked much younger; heavily built and getting heavier, for Congo life suited her! She was an incurable optimist, and just refused to see the dark side of anything. Not that she hid her head in the sand, but somehow she could always find something optimistic in every situation. A great talker and interested in people, nothing pleased her so much as having visitors with whom she could sit down and chat over a cup of tea or coffee.

She loved animals too, though her favourites were dogs, of which she had one, called rather inappropriately Simba. She loved him, and wherever Mary went, Simba usually followed.

Mary loved the Congolese and they in turn loved her, and respected her to a degree rarely found in our tribe. During the 1960 trouble when most of us were evacuated home, Mary stayed on alone at Bopepe and not once was arrested or questioned. Such was the esteem the population had for her.

Living with me, a Britisher, she adopted several of our habits, and the one we both liked best was the early morning cup of tea; it became as ritualistic with her as with me! Even when I was away she made it.

Such was my companion and senior missionary, with whom I worked from 1962 until November 1964.

The Simbas would call into Bopepe at any time, day or night, and Mary, though she had a natural fear of them, never showed it. Usually when they arrived, Mary's dog would rush out barking furiously, and Mary would then rush out yelling "Simba, Simba" to the dog; and to our amusement – the Simbas would answer, "Simba! Simba! Simba!" Then we would have to explain that Mary was only calling her dog. One Simba complained about the dog's name and suggested Mary change it, but she answered that the dog had been called by that name for seven years, and that the rebels had taken his name rather than he theirs!

We continued our evening prayer meetings with the villagers three times a week; then one night Pastor Bo Martin came and very sadly said they would hold the meeting in another house, and that we were not to go to it. Apparently the people were saying that we were holding political meetings, Mary, because she was American, being the proof. We realised then that we could be a liability to our friends, as continued friendship with us could be counted against them later, so we reluctantly had to acquiesce. As we prayed together that night, we read 2 Chronicles 20: 12, "O our God, wilt Thou not judge them? for we have no might against this great company that cometh against us, neither know we what to do; but our eyes are upon Thee"; and then on to the glorious answer in verse 15 – "The battle is not yours, but God's"; and again in verse 17 – "Ye shall not need to fight in this battle: set yourselves, stand ye still, and see the salvation of the Lord with you . . ." We quietly committed it all into the Father's hands.

Food began to be short, for we had been unable to buy supplies in August as expected; but it seemed that just when we were on the last tin, a parcel would arrive from headquarters in Stanleyville, usually brought by a very faithful friend who travelled on the mail bus. We had, of course, asked the Lord for supplies, but we certainly never expected European foods.

Happily we were both used to, and liked, Congolese food. Manioc and rice took the place of potatoes, and African spinach was one of our favourite vegetables. It had been one of my hobbies to raise chickens and now it paid off in that we had eggs and meat, though a Simba would come and demand two or three chickens at a time. By the time November came we had just two chickens left, and ten baby chicks. We often said we had eaten so much chicken, we could probably grow our own wings and fly home ourselves!

The Simbas came and took all our diesel oil with which we ran our electric motor, so one day in September we were without electricity and had to resort to kerosene lanterns. Then they came and relieved us of all but ten litres of our kerosene. It meant a strict economy in lights and the use of the refrigerator, though we were able to buy some from time to time from the local plantations.

We had several small hurricane lanterns and one large pressure lamp; the latter took too much kerosene, and also needed precious methylated spirits, and we decided to use it only for any grave emergency which might arise in the maternity or dispensary. Often it meant letting a patient wait over till daylight, when I could put in stitches or open an abcess, or probe a wound. The Lord gave grace even in this, and only once did I have a really serious case at night, which necessitated lighting the big lamp.

Then towards the end of September, we had to cut down even more and we would lay aside all work needing lights; we would light a log fire on the verandah, and sit around it until bedtime. We would pray together then (we could not read until we lit the lamps to go to bed), or watch the cars go by. When it was moonlight, Mary would play her accordion, accompanied by the two dogs who always howled whenever she played. The last time we did this was but a few days before our arrest, and Mary played "The Star-Spangled Banner" and "America the Beautiful". We both sang lustily, hoping there were no Simbas around and if there were, that they would not know the tunes!

Our house-boy, Fidele, was another problem. He was a man in his middle twenties, and had a wife and one child. He was extraordinarily clean and meticulous in his work, and his own home was kept as spick and span as ours. He was not naturally brave, and whenever a truck load of Simbas would drive into the village, Fidele would be out of the back door and into the forest like a flash! Poor fellow, it was not until later that we learned that his village were a hundred per cent M.N.C. (*Movement National Congolais*), the rebel political party, and each day when he went home he was harangued for working for the white people. He loved Mary, and had been her "boy" for seven years, and therefore had divided loyalties. He would listen to what they said they were going to do to the white people, so when the trucks came in he thought our end was coming, and took to his heels.

The third week in September, we had news via our trusted mail truck friend, about our colleague, Bill Scholten, a teacher from America, and also a most enthusiastic worker amongst young people; very tall and thin, he was almost a contrast to his short and pretty wife, and father of five quite young children. They had all lived and worked in our furthermost northwestern station of Ekoko, something like 300 to 400 miles from Stanleyville. We heard that Bill had been taken to prison and had died there. When we received the news, Bo Martin was very upset, as were we all, and Bo said he would go on his bicycle to Ekoko to see what had happened. We tried to talk him out of going, as it would only have meant trouble, but he was adamant: "Don't you realise that one of my brothers-in-the-Lord has died, and that it was one of my countrymen who killed him?" He was so ashamed. However, the village elders told him he could not go and leave us two women, as he had vowed he would protect us. He finally agreed to stay home, but it was evident that Bill's death had a depressing effect on Bo, indeed on all the villagers. How Bo prayed for Mrs. Scholten and the children! Many of the villagers, too, prayed for those who had been responsible for Bill's death. We redoubled our prayers for the Aketi Ekoko folk, as we had also heard various reports on the "grapevine" system of trouble in those areas.

Our tribal chief, called Mulaba Fidele, was the one who had promised us an animal from his herd for our conference and subsequently let us down. Apparently, he wanted a fantastic price for it, and the Africans had refused to allow him to exploit the white people. Now the Simbas were coming in every day and taking away three or four animals a day and not paying anything.

Chief Fidele had been nominally a Catholic, and though he went to Mass whenever the priest came round, he was not averse to coming to Bopepe Church for our services on a Sunday. He had received many threats from the Simbas, and looking around him decided it was time he put his soul right with the Lord. He sent for Bo Martin and talked long and earnestly with him, and Bo finally had the joy of leading him to the Lord Jesus Christ. The change in him was remarkable; from a weak and frightened man, he became a brave and decisive chief. He was greatly convicted about the animal business and said "I had refused to give God's people a cow, and now He has taken them all away."

One night after his conversion, he had a late visit from several trucks of Simbas, who told him to go out and call in the women to dance. At about 2.30 a.m. he was on his way home, when he met a messenger from his village who warned him not to return as the Simbas had made a plan to beat him up. The poor chief did not know what to do, or where to go, for to hide the chief would have meant death to any who were found with him in their house. He prayed then and there, and the Lord sent the answer in the form of a snake which bit him in the ankle! Now the answer was perfectly plain: he would have to go to the Bopepe dispensary for treatment, and therefore 3.15 a.m. found a very sick man on our verandah. I only had one ampoule of anti-snake venom serum left, so with much prayer that this would be sufficient, I gave it to him, and Bo Martin said he would lodge him in his house. He became seriously ill, his glands were swollen all over his body and he was in much pain. Only the prayers of the Lord's people saved his life, I am sure.

Whilst he was in Bo's house, he would spend hours on end reading his Bible, saying he did not realise how much he had missed all these years by not reading it. He stayed with us at Bopepe for two weeks in all, and Bo was able to help him spiritually. He became one of our strongest friends when the days became more and more difficult. I do not know what has since happened to him, but I feel sure he would have conducted himself as a true Christian.

Often the Simbas would call into Bopepe for food or something else. One day when they came it was pouring with rain, as only it can in the Congo; three Simbas came on to the verandah, one of them just a young boy of perhaps nine or ten years of age. He was shirtless and soaking wet; he had his magic medicine on, and carried a rifle. I asked him if he was really a Simba or a mascot (how naïve can I be?). He drew himself up to his full height and informed me he was an officer, an adjutant, and what was more, a doctor to the rebel army! He stood there shivering as though he had malarial chills; at least I knew their magic medicine did not stop them from feeling the cold. Poor kids, we felt so sorry for them when they climbed back into their open truck. They were probably hungry and tired, though at that stage, not yet disillusioned.

As the People's Army is fed by the people, the villagers used to take it in turns to take food in twice a week, and then the women would have to stop and sing and dance all day. It was always a sore point with the other villages that the Bopepe women would not stay to dance; also the fact that not one young man from Bopepe had joined the People's Army. Consequently, when the people or Simbas passed our village, we came in for a lot of abuse and threats, how that we were all reactionaries, and Bo Martin was preaching against the rebels, and how the school teachers were "eating" all the money which should be shared between the people, and how the two white people were spies for Tshombe's government. It was not a happy environment, yet we all found we could find real peace in the Lord, and the worse the threats, the deeper the peace.

Mary used to take religious instruction in school, but finally had to give it up due to pressure from parents, especially those who were in the M.N.C. villages. Mary was quite upset by this, and all we could do was to pray for the little ones, that their minds would not be poisoned by it all.

Each week, Paul Ponea would come to us with a new list of names of boys who had joined up. Several were only nine- or ten-year-olds, of whom one later became our guard whilst we were in prison, and later almost a personal bodyguard for me. The big Simbas respected the *petits Simbas* as they were called.

Often trucks packed full of Simbas would go by us. Usually they would be singing their songs of hate, which whilst having beautiful melodies, would have terrible words. Sadly we would watch them go, young boys, armed with machetes and spears and clubs, going to war against modern arms; what chance would they have? Our hearts just ached for them, young manhood going to a virtual suicide for a dying cause. Mary would pray that the wheel of the truck would come off, or else that they would run out of gasoline, "Anything, Lord, to stop them arriving at the place of battle."

When they called in at Bopepe, quite often they would ask us to pray for them, and we could quite honestly say we had prayed for them every day – but we did not add *how* we had prayed!

Sometime in October, a Captain arrived in a truck. He was a believer, but by virtue of his being ex-military had been forced to join the rebel army. He called to ask if he could be baptised as he felt sure he would die in battle. He had left Buta with twenty-five wounded on his truck; when he arrived at Bopepe, ninety-five miles away, all but four had died en route, and of these, one was almost dead. It was arranged that on his return he should be baptised. This was done about a week later, and we all gathered in the church afterwards for communion. He never returned from the war.

One evening as we sat on the verandah, two men came along on bicycles and stopped outside our house. They came up to us, and as we had stood to greet them, they then promptly sat down in our chairs, and left us standing! They had cycled in from Banalia, and were civilians, but members of the Rebel political party, M.N.C. The father of one of them had sent them along to us in order to sell us their political party card; they had a new model. We politely refused the offer, explaining that we were missionaries and not interested in politics. The one whose father had sent him leaned over and said very quickly, "There is a very bad time coming for you white people; it would be wise to buy one, it may be the means of saving your life." We

42

had heard about Gbenye's scorched earth policy, and the threats to the white people via the radio, and wondered just what was the threat behind the words of our visitor. However, we insisted that we did not wish to buy a card, and they eventually left us. When Bo Martin came over to tell us the news bulletin from Leopoldville, and we him about the B.B.C. news, he said we had done the right thing, but it was plain to see that he was very disturbed. Poor Bo, he missed his twin brother during these days. Pastor Asani was up country in A.I.M. territory, with his wife and two catechists. I heard later he had crossed the border into Uganda and subsequently flown to Leopoldville, but at the time of the story we did not know if he was alive or not. Bo had dreamed that he saw his twin brother in another country. We were glad Pastor Asani was not with us, as he would certainly have run the gauntlet of the rebels' wrath.

Because both Bo Martin and Pastor Asani lived at Bopepe and had associations with white people, and because they dressed neatly, spoke French fluently, and in the case of Pastor Asani had received training in Europe, they were both suspected of being reactionaries, and belonging to the other political party. Word was brought to us that the administration at Banalia were combing the lists of the other party in order to find the twins' names, but Bo happily said that their names would not be found as they had not joined that party.

Feelings ran high about the twins, and all sorts of false accusations were made against them. Bo was fearless in his preaching, so much so, that we felt constrained to warn him not to preach against the movement, but to keep to the pure word of God. Our fears were realised when one day he was called to Banalia to answer a charge that he had preached against Lumumba – the late Prime Minister, assassinated in 1961 – saying he was a devil. Actually Bo had not mentioned Lumumba by name, but had preached on "Thou shalt have no other gods beside Me" (Exodus 20).

43

One Sunday morning whilst we were in church, we heard a truck stop outside, and within minutes, the Simbas were in the church, with their rifles at the ready; they came through all the doors, and looked very menacing. The preacher had stopped speaking, and several women began to weep. They were looking for the white nurse, as one of their members had toothache and wanted some aspirins! I was only too happy to comply with this request, and went off with the suffering Simba and several others, whilst Mary whispered to a Simba who was near her, that if they would like a drink, she would make it for them, if they would come to her house. Anything to get them out of the church. They agreed, and left with her. Outside, one boy of about fourteen emptied his rifle into a tree, which also had the effect of emptying the church of women. Their delight in frightening people knew no bounds.

The Simbas who were having a drink were in our sitting-room, and as one of them received his, he took off his hat and returned thanks to God; another crossed himself. They were mostly young boys, between the ages of fourteen and eighteen years. One had been educated at our school in Wanie Rukula; he asked if he might sit in on the rest of the service. Several came back into the church with us, and shared our Bibles and hymn books, and appeared to be quite at home in the church. They are a strange mixture, the rebels.

One evening as we were talking together on the verandah, we discussed the subject of death. Mary said that we had died to self years ago, else we would never have come to the Congo in the first place, and any subsequent death would be merely physical, for if we regarded ourselves as dead, it did not matter what happened to our bodies, our souls were assured of continuance of life with the Lord which was far better. She quoted Paul's reference – 2 Corinthians 1 : 9 – "But we had the sentence of death in ourselves . . ."

The last week in October, a plane flew over very high during the evening. Rumours spread about that the white people were calling the planes; at the same time Gbenye Christophe, the self-styled Prime Minister and "President" of the rebels, decided to collect hostages. On Thursday, October 29th, several trucks passed Bopepe on their way to the plantations, to arrest all the planters. The missionaries were exempt ... but for how long?

The following day we heard the trucks coming along the road. I was at the dispensary and ran out to watch them go by; our neighbours and friends were on them, with their wives and children, and we waved to each other. It was very difficult to concentrate on our work after that, and as for eating, our appetites just left us. We wondered if ever we would meet again.

We repacked our evacuation cases with things we might need for a long stay in prison, though at the same time, hoping we would not have to go.

We continued in this state of tension for several days. We would pray, but there was no release in it. During those intervening days we had to face up to the possibility of not only imprisonment, but death also.

The last Sunday Bo Martin preached fearlessly on Ephesians 6 – "Put on the whole armour of God." We both had the presentiment that this was to be our last Sunday at Bopepe and we were not alone in this, for the attitude of the people made it obvious that they too felt it. They were extra loving, many brought gifts, and some were even tearful. All day long we had visits from various ones who wanted to come just to shake hands, and they would sit in a bleak silence on the verandah looking at us sadly and cracking their finger-joints, always a sign that they were uneasy. Occasionally they would let out "*Omaou*", which is a word indicating distress.

That evening Mary played her accordion for a long time. Neither of us spoke; it somehow eased our pent-up feelings to hear the well-known hymns again, each one with its own particular nostalgia. Before we went to bed, as we prayed together, Mary had a hard time controlling her tears.

Monday and Tuesday passed in the same state of tension; the traffic on the road was heavier, several truck-loads of Simbas went by to the battle areas, several came back containing their wounded, usually with a blood-stained spear tied to the front of the car.

Tuesday night we went to bed as usual after hearing the ten o'clock news from B.B.C. – nothing about Congo again. The mail truck failed to arrive, though that was nothing out of the ordinary.

At 11.30 p.m. Mary heard a truck coming along the road; it stopped outside Bopepe village, and thinking it might be the mail truck, Mary went out on to the verandah to meet the friend who always travelled on it. Imagine her shock to find six half-naked Simbas on the verandah, all with spears, their bodies decorated with palm leaves and their magic medicine!

"Get back into the house, white lady, you are under arrest" – Mary hastily complied with the order, and called out to me to get up, we had visitors . . .

3

In Prison

WHEN I heard Mary call that we had visitors, I knew immediately what type, as I could hear their demands from my room. Hastily putting on my housecoat and lighting a hurricane lamp, and at the same time praying for guidance and wisdom, I went out to meet them.

There they were, half-naked with palm fronds on their heads and chests, grasping spears, leering at us. Their spokesman said he had come to inspect the house and take us to Banalia. He saw young Julienne, a child from the village, in bed, and demanded to know who she was and said she must get up. Bless her heart, she was still sound asleep ... I shook her violently, and when she saw the Simbas she almost fell out of bed! The Simbas were most impressed that we had given her a real European bed, with sheets and blankets just like the white people have! Poor Julienne was wearing one of my night-dresses and was acutely embarrassed to be found standing in front of all these men so inadequately dressed. Sensing her embarrassment, I found her cloth and she hastily wound it around herself.

She was a brave kid, only fifteen, but did not falter at all except when the Simbas accused her of having lived an immoral life, when she just flared up and lashed them with her tongue and eyes.

The Simbas were both tired and hungry, and with true Virginian hospitality, Mary offered to feed them. We only had two tins of sardines left and some rice, and she explained our poverty. They understood and told her to open only one tin of

47

sardines and to keep the other for ourselves. We ushered Julienne into the kitchen out of sight of the men. Mary then asked if the girl could be allowed to go home to her mother, as she had done nothing wrong, and was only sleeping in our house to ease the housing situation in her own. They agreed to let her go, and she just walked calmly down the hill and went home as though she was used to that kind of life.

After about an hour we heard Bo Martin at the door, and it was then we realised that two of the Simbas had gone to his house to arrest him too. They had searched his house from top to bottom for the inevitable transmitter radio they thought we all possessed. The food, when ready, was placed on the table with some coffee, and the Simbas ate hungrily. They had allowed us to cook it as they said we were "good women" and did not live immoral lives.

After they had eaten, they then wanted to search the house. They went to my room and the first thing they saw was my little transistor radio with the aerial up – that was taken immediately, and I had to demonstrate how it worked. Very quickly I moved the station from the B.B.C. to Stanleyville. ... it would not have done for them to have heard English being spoken! The radio was also marked with a pencil at the B.B.C. and Leopoldville stations, so whilst making out that the markings were difficult to see in the poor light, I was able to erase them.

The Simbas were tired and decided to leave the house inspection until morning. They gave us permission to go to bed. Mary's room was off the living-room and she did not fancy being there, so she asked permission to put Julienne's bed, which was a folding type, in my room; they allowed us to do that. Bo Martin sat in a chair all night talking to them. He attempted several times to preach to them, but each time they refused to listen.

We of course, did not sleep. We lay on our beds and whispered to each other, then we prayed, and never has a night seemed so long. At last 5.30 a.m. came and we hastily washed, dressed, and packed our cases with last minute things.

Would the Simbas like a cup of tea? Yes, and so we all had one. Bo Martin was allowed to go back to his home with an escort, but returned after fifteen minutes.

We asked the Simbas what the programme would be for the day. The house would be inspected from top to bottom, then we could eat, and then we would all go to Banalia. If a truck came, by truck; if not, on foot. Our hearts sank. "This is it," we said.

At 6.30 they asked why we had not gone to church. They then promptly dispatched all three of us to go. Bo took that last service. I cannot remember what he spoke about at all, but I know the last hymn was the Bangala version of "Fight the good fight", and how difficult it was to sing with a lump in my throat, and tears in my eyes. After that service nobody came to shake hands or to greet us; they were all too upset . . .

Back at the house they began our "inspection"; Mary began with her room, all six Simbas crowded in, and Bo Martin had to be present as well. The mattress was even lifted, but of course, we had nothing to hide. Next came my room; again everything had to be explained, and any medical equipment was examined over and over again, especially my auroscope which I had brought from the dispensary in case I needed it for odd callers who would come for treatment after the dispensary was closed. My books were a source of astonishment, for I had so many. Due to lack of space, I kept most of them in a trunk and a case; they were all carefully looked at for titles, but as they were for the most part in English, the Simbas were none the wiser. So we went through the house, the office, the bathroom, the living-room, dining-room, kitchen; nothing was spared the scrutiny of six pairs of inquisitive brown eyes. In the attic they found the remains of an old tape recorder, and also a transformer. The latter they were convinced was a transmitter; they had never heard of a transformer and were none

49

the wiser when informed. Well, it was very heavy, and if they wanted to carry it all the way to Banalia, that was up to them.

By this time our house-boy had arrived, and was told by the Simbas to feed us. The Simbas then left the house to supervise a meal being cooked for them by the schoolgirls.

We sat down to a breakfast of coffee and bread and marmalade, but the bread tasted like sawdust and we could not get more than half a slice down. The leader of the Simbas was very upset at this, and pleaded with us to eat more as we had a long day ahead of us. We tried again, but it was no use.

Having obtained permission to go to my little hospital, I went, intending to give the last treatment to all the in-patients, but I need not have bothered. The hospital was empty; they had all fled. Very sadly I locked the doors. Somehow we felt so apart from our people. They, of course, were too scared to come near us. On the way back I met one of the teachers; he had often helped me with my chickens, and I gave him permission to eat them or keep them as he felt best. Bless him, he was so sure it would only be for a few days, he refused to take them, but said he would keep his eye on them.

The villagers were standing about in little groups, some women had their hands on their heads, one of the signs of grief. We were unable to speak to them, to comfort them. *Daily Light* that morning had been very topical for us; November 4th, morning reading – "Now for a season, if need be, ye are in heaviness through manifold temptations"; "Beloved think it not strange concerning the fiery trial which is to try you . . ." and so on, right down the page. As we prayed together that morning, those words brought wonderful peace and comfort to our hearts. It was all right, all that was happening was in the permissive will of God, somehow we were rid of the responsibility, it was all His.

The Simbas wanted very much to take my radio, but under their laws it had to be given, so I had to sign a piece of paper stating that they had my full permission to take it . . . In many ways we were glad to see it go, for it had been quite a liability, especially when we listened to radio Leopoldville: one of us had to sit outside to watch for Simbas or visitors who might report us.

Eventually 10 a.m. came, with of course no sign of a truck; it was therefore evident that we were going to have to walk the fifteen miles to Banalia, and as it was the dry season, we knew it would be a hot, cloudless day. What about our cases? Here we were, two helpless white women, who were unused to carrying heavy loads even short distances! The Lord had it all planned out for us; Paul Ponea and another teacher, Ndama Gregoire, volunteered to carry our cases on the back of their bicycles all the way to Banalia; then we also had many friends who wanted to carry our handbags and lamps for us, and so we were virtually empty-handed.

With heavy hearts we set out on that long walk to Banalia. The village folk lined the pathway from the village via the dispensary; many were crying quite openly, many turned their backs on us as we passed, another sign of great sorrow. A few took our hands in both of theirs and whispered "God bless", or "God go with you". Mary, dear soul, was able to find the composure to answer them all, but I dared not trust myself to say a word, my heart was too full. Once on the main road, we started out at a brisk pace, and the drums sent messages ahead. At each village large groups were gathered on the roadway to greet us, or to weep. The womenfolk in particular astonished me, by the vehement way they rounded upon the Simbas for taking away their two "Mamas". Before the day was through we were even feeling sorry for the Simbas!

The Simbas honoured us in allowing us to head the procession, for such it was with the various people who carried our things and those who walked with us in order to identify themselves with us. Sometimes we would hear an argument behind us, and find some new folk who wanted to be allowed to carry our things.

Somewhere in the crowd was Bo Martin; he was kept with the Simbas all the time. As we passed the chief's village, the chief was there to meet us. With a face like thunder he took our proffered hands in both of his, and without a word, but with tears in his eyes, just bowed low over them; how this man was to fight for our release, we did not then know.

We stopped every two or three miles at the order of the leading Simba, in order for Mary to rest. He commanded chairs and refreshment to be brought, but we did not have appetite for anything.

On the way we talked together of the sufferings of the Lord, and we reminded each other of the various promises in the Word; it was rather like the Emmaus Road experience, for surely He walked with us and our hearts burned within us. The two boys with the baggage on their bicycles left the things near Banalia then cycled back, and the Simbas gave us permission to ride ahead and wait for them at the other end. I was so glad, for Mary's feet were beginning to be very sore, and our resting places seemed to be more and more frequent – or was it that the miles seemed to be longer and longer? We cycled until I nearly fell off my bicycle with faintness, and rested at a village where we had sugar cane and corn and bananas, and lovely cool water. Thus fortified, we cycled on to one mile before Banalia, where we waited for the party to catch up with us. The villagers all along the road were incensed at our arrest, but also very frightened, though there were women from each group who spoke their minds freely to the Simbas.

By 4.30 p.m. we were all together again, and to our astonishment the Simbas said we would wait until 5.30, explaining that by that time most of the Simbas in Banalia would be in camp and there would be less chance of our being molested. We were very grateful for this thoughtfulness and had cause to praise the Lord for it even more when four days later, the Sharpes arrived in Banalia during the morning and we saw the way they were received.

At 5.30 we passed the final barrier and were at last on the ferry. We were beautifully sunburned, though my nose was a brilliant red and became the butt of jokes for days to come!

As we were crossing we saw a crowd gradually collecting on the landing stage. As we stepped off, a mob of young Simbas came and surrounded us, brandishing their spears and threatening terrible things. Suddenly we heard our Simba leader say something in his own tribal language; all the Simbas stepped back, and our own original six came round us, two in front, and behind, and one each side. Our leader said very gently to us, "Don't be afraid, we are responsible for you, and we will not let these people touch you; only stay within our guard."

Amidst the catcalls of the others we marched off to the headquarters, one of the European houses which had been commandeered by the Simbas. Our leader came to attention and gave his report, which was very much in our favour, and we were shown into a room which had obviously been a beautiful lounge, but was now filthy and wrecked by the Simbas. Bo joined us. We too were filthy, from the dust on the road, and absolutely exhausted both physically and mentally. The time was 6 p.m.

Bo Martin was now released. He had apparently only been brought along as a chaperon for us, as we had not any menfolk of our own. He continued to sit with us as our papers were examined. None of us spoke, we were too busy with our own thoughts.

Whilst waiting, we heard that a similar escort party to ours had been sent to Bodela for the Parrys, and another to Bongondza for the Sharpes. We livened up immediately at the thought of seeing these folk again.

Our identity cards were kept by the Simbas, but our passports returned. We had an apologetic word from the commander of the base, who read to us the orders he had received from Stanleyville to arrest us all, though we were not to be beaten or killed.

We were taken to a building we had often noticed when in Banalia; it was right on the main road and gave a commanding view of the river. The house was devoid of furniture save a wooden settee and a small round coffee table. We did a tour of inspection. Ugh! it was filthy. The bathroom lacked water, the toilet not only lacked water but had been used by the entire army it seemed. The stench was nauseating even to me, and I pride myself that as a trained nurse I can stand anything. Bo Martin came with us and he was appalled at this state of affairs, and said he would go and see what he could do for us. Whilst he was gone, eight or nine Belgian planters and their wives were ushered in, and the Simbas brought in chairs for us all. They sat round in glum silence. I asked one woman how long she had been a prisoner and she said three days; she rightly guessed we had just arrived by my sunburned nose.

Bo came back with several officers and also the civilian who was responsible for the upkeep (or otherwise) of the houses. From another house they produced a bedstead and a very hard, lumpy mattress which only covered one-third of the bed. Dear Bo was upset about this, and demanded something better for his two *demoiselles*. The arguments became very heated, and Mary pleaded with Bo not to antagonise the Simbas, but he was dauntless, and went on and on until the Simba officer called to the *jeunesse* who were guarding us to take him prisoner and put him in the *calshot* (solitary confinement) all night. He was run out of the house, and later we heard they had made him run all round Banalia at spear-point before finally shutting him up in the even filthier prison block. To be in the *calshot* meant to the Simbas standing to attention over an open privy for hours on end without a light. Usually shoes were taken off, and as the ground around the privy was not very sanitary, it was not a very pleasant occupation. During the night they relented and pushed him into a damp dark single cell, and according to Bo, he took his coat off and made a pillow, and then after long hours of prayer, he lay down on the damp cold floor and went to sleep.

Mary pleaded with the officer to have mercy on Bo, explaining he was only trying to look after us, but they were adamant, saying he was a reactionary and trying to shield the white people.

Our distress was great, and all we could do was silently commit our brother to the care and keeping of the Lord.

After about an hour, the Parrys arrived; they were absolutely exhausted, but obviously overjoyed to meet us. They had not been so well favoured as us. The Simbas had arrived at six that morning, and had given them exactly five minutes to leave. The children, aged ten and eight, were still in pyjamas, though Dennis and Nora were dressed. The coffee was on the table and Nora was in the process of mixing the milk (we have powdered milk) when the Simbas arrived; they would not even let them drink their coffee!

Permission was granted for the children to dress, and Dennis snatched what he could and packed it into two small cases. By 6.40 they were on the road. The rebels refused to allow anyone to carry the Parrys' cases, and in fact made them carry the Simbas' baggage as well as their own! They tormented them along the way, hitting the children on the head with their spears, though Nora warned both not to cry as it would only aggravate the situation. They made Grace carry things on her head as the Congolese do, and of course she could not, so they hit her again, but she did not cry. The Simbas would race on ahead and drink the native wine, and were soon quite drunk. When a halt was called on the way, the Parrys were made to stand in the hot sunshine. No food or drink was offered them, and the people were too afraid to help them.

Once Grace wanted to go to the toilet and permission was grudgingly given but a Simba insisted on going along. He was halfway there, when he was called back and reminded that Congolese men do not go with womenfolk under such conditions; he sheepishly returned.

After about seven miles, Nora collapsed into a deep faint.

The Simbas were frightened and carried her into a house and left her with the womenfolk of the village. Somebody was sent ahead to Banalia for transport, but it was almost six hours before it came, a tractor and trailer. In the meantime the children were made to prepare food for the Simbas, and humiliated when they made mistakes. Grace was made to dance. When the food was at long last ready, they gave the entire family a plantain (a cooked banana) apiece. The children ate ravenously, but Nora and Dennis were not hungry and gave theirs to Andrew.

They eventually arrived in Banalia about 6.30 p.m. and came to our place of imprisonment about 7.30. Nora, never robust at the best of times, looked terrible, and the children were too tired to talk. I took off their coats, and Grace's shoes; her feet were all blistered.

We had packed a loaf of bread and a tin of sardines and these were made into sandwiches; the children ate well, but we adults were not very hungry, though we ate as it was obviously the wisest thing to do. Water was brought from somewhere, but it was finished in no time . . .

Young Grace was inclined to whimper, but we whispered to her to try and be brave as otherwise the Simbas would be mad at us. Poor little bewildered girl . . . she had suffered emotionally that day enough to send an adult crazy, but instead she clutched my hand and whispered that she had asked Jesus to make her brave.

Our lamps were lit, and the Simbas arranged themselves by the door to goad us; we tried not to listen but it was very hard. We were all desperately tired and very uncomfortable, as there were still no toilet facilities. The Simbas began singing their war songs, and generally being very offensive.

By this time, various articles of furniture had been brought in, and a large African-type bed-frame was laid on the floor in one corner, and a mattress-less bedstead in another. We put Nora on the bedstead, and Mary, Grace and I laid on the other thing in the opposite corner. Dennis and Andrew stretched out on the settee, but were constantly badgered by the Simbas. Little Grace whimpered, and would sit up every half an hour or so, saying, "Where is Daddy?" or, "What are they saying to Daddy?" I prayed with her very quietly and almost in her ear. She clutched my hand all night.

The night was cold and we did not have any blankets, but one of the planters had, and he lent us a blanket and Nora a sheet. The planters stretched out where they were, or on the floor; some even snored!

During that long, cold, uncomfortable night, a youngish Simba came to me, and kneeling at my head (I was practically at floor level), whispered. He asked if I was a Protestant missionary, and then asked if I could show him how to accept Christ as his own personal Saviour. He spoke in Bangala, but had a Swahili Gospel of John. I could not move from my position, nor did he want me to speak out loud, so lying flat on my back talking to a Simba who was at my head, it was a great joy, more so maybe because of our conditions, to show him the way of salvation through the Scriptures. He prayed very simply, handing over his life and soul to Christ, and I prayed afterwards. We did not realise then how he was going to be able to help us in the days which followed.

Next morning we rose very stiffly and shook ourselves. There was no water and we had to make use of the nauseating toilet facilities – there was no alternative. We read and prayed together, though I cannot recall what we read.

There was still no news of the Sharpes and Ruby; we wondered what was happening to them. We knew that neither Audrey nor Andy could walk very far. Audrey had broken a bone in her foot, and had only had the plaster of Paris off one week, and Andy had very bad motor co-ordination of his legs, due to spasticity, though he could walk, and would probably be game to play his part; but he *was* only four years old.

Bo Martin was still in prison; the Commandant came and

Mary pleaded with him to release him, and to our astonishment he said he would.

The boys who had carried our things on their bicycles later came and told us that Bo had been released and was in the Commandant's office. The planters were sent to a different place and we were left in this awful house. We asked about sanitation and the Simbas promised to help and did, in fact, sort it all out before the day was through. They even filled the bath with water, but the plug did not fit very well, and in two hours it had all disappeared. We also had a bucket which had many holes, and if one was quick enough one could carry water from the bath to the toilet, but it was practically necessary to do the four-minute mile speed!

We had water, Bo was released; our next problem was food, not for us, but for the children. Andrew would cheerfully announce, "Say, but I'm hungry", at half-hourly intervals. For an active, growing boy of ten he was bound to be hungry. The Congolese boys who had come with us went to Banalia village about a mile away, where the U.F.M. had a district church with an evangelist and his wife. They came back in the late afternoon with a steaming bowl of rice and chicken, some bananas and a pineapple. We then realised how hungry we all were.

There were no plates or spoons, in fact none of the refinements of our age, so after we had given thanks we all dug in with our fingers into the communal bowl . . . We laughed almost hysterically at the sight we must have presented to the continuous stream of onlookers who were always at the windows and doors.

Still no news of the Sharpes and Ruby. We asked the Commandant for news, and he said he too was worried and if they had not come by morning he would personally go to find them.

We only had one lamp between us now, and the Simbas insisted on having it, therefore there was only one thing to do at sundown – go to bed, such as it was . . . When the planters left we had re-explored the house and found a room with two single beds and one lumpy mattress, and another room with a three-quarter size bed and a tiny leaf mattress. The Parrys took the two-bedded room, and we the other. After a time of reading and prayer, we separated to our rooms.

We pushed our mattress into the middle of the bed, and decided to "top and tail" – it would have been funny under different circumstances, but we were too tired to care, and we mercifully slept most of the night, though wakened very early in the morning through cold, as there were no bedclothes and, though we had not undressed, it was still very cold. We lay there whispering in the dark.

At long last daylight came and we were able to get up. We washed in a cupful of water and combed our hair, feeling much better for the night's sleep. Dennis led us in family worship.

There were a few bananas and the pineapple, and we ate the former and saved the latter for when we should be hungry later.

Bo came to see us, and said he would go back to Bopepe and send in blankets and equipment for eating, etc. He also made arrangements with the local evangelist and his wife to feed us twice a day, and we gave him money so that they could buy food from the market. We watched him cycle away with the other boys. Whilst he had been around, we had felt we had somebody to help; now we felt alone.

During that morning we were thrilled to see several of the Bopepe women coming to see us, each carrying a bundle on her head. When the Simbas gave permission, they came in to us. They had collected amongst themselves and had received enough money to buy rice and peanuts and four chickens. They brought along enough for two or three days, and promised to come every other day. We were very moved by this lovely gesture on their part, which showed the outward witness of an indwelling Christ. We sat and talked, and when the women left, they wept. They had cycled in from Bopepe, setting out at 5 a.m., a whole hour before daybreak.

Later that same day we were to see an angry mob, and witness how mob violence is conducted. It was 2.30 p.m. We had nothing to do, and were just sitting quietly talking, and Andrew was teasing Grace as only boys can tease a sister younger than they, when a truck of singing Simbas turned into Banalia past our "prison-house". We heard it screech to a stop; we heard the cry, "Where are the white people?" and our stomachs contracted and our mouths went dry. We could only pray for help.

They came and surrounded the house, absolutely mad at us. A youngster of about eleven or twelve years old, but very loquacious, stood in the doorway — our guards had fled — and turning his back on us, addressed the now rapidly growing crowd. He told how white people were fighting (the rebels had just lost another town to the National Army), how the white women were also joining the National Army and he personally had seen lots of Simbas shot down and killed by white women ... *We* knew it was untrue, but the crowd wanted to believe anything, and they did. We were ordered out of the house — "Get your things and go to Stanleyville," they yelled. We rushed and grabbed our things, separated from each other by the mob. I was surrounded, with several spears digging in my ribs, and I know the others had the same treatment. I was forced to run carrying my heavy suitcase; "*Mateka*, that's what you are, *mateka, mateka, mateka*," they kept saying, accompanying it with gestures of cutting throats. Strangely enough, fear left me and I was able to answer them, though rather out of breath, "Oh, that's fine, I'm ready to die, but what about you? Are you ready?" — but this only made them angrier. I caught a glimpse of Nora ahead of me, but could not see the children, or Dennis or Mary.

Suddenly in the midst of all the confusion, a loud voice was heard yelling, "Not the missionaries, they're Protestants, send them back." We were turned round and allowed to return at our own pace. Most of the crowd then left us in order to harass the planters, but even so we still had several around us,

60

of whom one was a child of about ten years of age. He was dressed in a monkey-skin hat, and had fur on his wrists, and the usual medicine charms around his neck; he carried a spear, the handle of which was cut down to size. He smiled, and I noticed that not all of his upper molars were through — strange the things one notices under such conditions. He then asked, "Aren't you Mademoiselle Margarita from Bopepe?" and when I nodded he added, "You delivered my mother last time — you're good. And that woman over there," pointing to Mary, "isn't she Beka?" (Beka was how they pronounced Baker, and Mary seldom had "Mademoiselle" attached.) Again I nodded. "She once took my mother in her car to the Banalia hospital before you had a place at Bopepe — she's a good woman too. Why are you here? You've not done anything wrong."

We reached the house absolutely exhausted. The little Simba immediately made himself our guard, and very effective he was too. The house was surrounded by Simbas, peering in at every window, some with obscene gestures, some mimicking a throat being cut, but all brandishing their spears. None of us felt very brave, but our main concern was for Grace; she was ashen, and on the verge of hysteria. Dennis suggested we prayed with our eyes open, literally "praying and watching". As he prayed, so we calmed down inside too, and eventually Grace settled down quietly also.

Our self-constituted guard of ten years old found another youngster of about fourteen and a youth of maybe nineteen, to stand in with him, and thanks to his authoritative attitude, the crowd dispersed.

We heard a shout and saw the truck go past the window, packed tight with war-happy Simbas chanting and, sitting or standing, the other white folk who had left us the day before. The women were so white we wondered what their fate would be, and even to this day I still do not know if any of them lost their lives in Stanleyville.

We were hungry, and regretted sending all the peanuts to

the village to be cooked; we had not eaten since 9.30 a.m. and it was now 4.30 p.m. We knew if nothing came by five o'clock we would be hungry until the following morning, as there was a curfew for civilians from 5 p.m. to 7 a.m. No food came. We literally tightened our belts; we felt bad for the children's sake, especially Andrew, as he had a healthy boy's appetite, but not once did he complain, and as night fell, after a time of prayer together, we went to our rooms, ostensibly to sleep.

Suddenly the door of our room was opened and one of the original Simbas who had arrested us burst in, saying that a V.I.P. had come and would probably come and see the white people; adding for our comfort, that he was a very hard man and would probably shout and scream at us, but if we were polite, he, the Simba, would speak well on our behalf. He also added very quietly that the Sharpes were just the other side of Bopepe, and would arrive in the morning.

We thanked God for positive news of Ian and Audrey and committed them once again to His care. We wondered who the V.I.P. was, and lay there on our mattress, top to tail, balancing precariously, when we heard the outside doors open and Simbas being interrogated by somebody evidently in authority. We heard the footsteps going to the Parrys' room, and Grace's scream of terror as she awakened from sleep and saw the room full of people.

What does one pray in situations like this? It is so difficult to voice thoughts when one's heart is pounding and racing at an incredible speed, and ears are strained for sounds. I prayed quietly to myself, "This is an S.O.S., Father, we need your help," and found myself saying it over and over again; Mary was repeating to herself, "We're in Your hands, Lord, we're in Your hands."

The door opened and suddenly the small room was filled with people with lamps. Blinded by the sudden light, I struggled to sit up – I have always felt it *infra dig* to lie in bed when people are in the room, and in this situation we must have looked a sight, Mary's feet by my head, and mine at her head, both of us clutching the mattress to stop ourselves rolling off ... One of the V.I.P.'s (there were two) had a radio in his arms, which was playing the cha-cha-cha so beloved by these Simbas.

He did not bother to turn it down, but spoke above the noise of it. He politely listened whilst "our" Simba made his report, then asked us several questions. He said we were not to worry and that he would try and find us more suitable accommodation. Then, taking the light with them, they all filed out, the door was shut, and all became quiet.

He was as good as his word, and next day we were allowed to use his house during the day, but had to return in the evening. He had a clean home, well furnished, with a bathroom. We were grateful for this respite from our squalid conditions. The Sharpes and Ruby still did not arrive, and the Commandant, accompanied by the V.I.P. of the night before, who turned out to be the Civil Administrator, went by truck to find them.

The day passed quietly enough. Food was brought at 10 a.m., with the promise of more at 2 p.m. They had brought fried bananas, which were still hot even though the village was a mile away.

There were several visits from Simbas who wanted to tell us what they personally thought of the white race, and Protestant missionaries in particular, but when they became too abusive, our guards would make them leave.

Mary used to wear one of those chains on her spectacles, which enabled her to have them with her all the time. The clips with which it was fastened were large and ornate; we heard the Simbas discussing them and saying it was a secret radio. So Mary very wisely removed the chain and left it behind in the Administrator's house.

They decided we had with us drugs and weapons with which to take our own lives, and even though we had explained that this was against all our principles as Christians, they insisted on searching our baggage. They relieved us of anything that had a point – pins, needles, nail scissors, nail file, two knives and the tin opener. They even wanted Mary's hair pins; she had long hair, and wore it in a bun. She asked what she was to do with her hair, and they asked why could she not tie it round her neck ... We laughed so much at this ridiculous statement that they realised they had made fools of themselves, and gave back the pins. They also took our aspirins and anti-malarial drugs, but said we could have them as needed on request.

On Sunday, November 8th, at about 9 a.m., the party from Bongondza arrived. We were thrilled to see them at long last! They were filthy, covered in the thick red dust from the road, sunburned, tired and hungry.

They had been arrested on November 4th, and had had to go by foot to Kole, fifteen miles away. As neither Audrey nor Andrew were able to walk very far, the Christians loaned them their bicycles, pushing them all the way. When they reached Kole, they were rewarded by being struck across the face for helping the white people.

On arrival at Kole, it was discovered that the doctor was supposed to have brought all his equipment with him, as well as any food he would need. Therefore Ian Sharpe went back with Ruby Gray, on bicycles, accompanied by Simbas, to do the necessary packing, and a truck followed to pick up all the goods.

Meanwhile Audrey and the three children, Jillian, aged eight, Alison, seven, and Andrew, four, waited at Kole. They were not given anywhere to lie down or rest, only a form on which to sit; nobody thought to feed them. They were there for twenty-four hours. Audrey said the children slept most of the night on the floor.

Also arrested at the same time was the Bongondza Pastor, Masini Phillipe, a great warrior for the Lord. His son, Mbongo Samuel, should also have been arrested, but he was away. They therefore took his wife and baby as hostages until he arrived.

With them also was the Sharpes' house-boy, Tele Gaston, who refused to leave the party. The two men were cruelly tied and beaten.

Eventually Ian and Ruby and the truck arrived at Kole. Ian was ordered to take off his shoes and socks, and the Simbas surrounded him, dancing and yelling and brandishing their spears. Suddenly one of the officers appeared on the scene and demanded to know why they were treating the doctor in this way. He was allowed to put on his shoes and socks again, and the entire party boarded the truck bound for Banalia, fifty miles away.

At one place on their journey they were made to dismount and both Ian and Audrey were struck across the face, but the Simba who struck them was immediately set upon by the other Simbas, and very cruelly beaten.

They arrived at Banalia on Sunday morning, November 8th, having been four days coming approximately seventy miles. We were in the Administrator's house when they came and they were only too pleased to utilise the bathroom facilities for a thorough clean up.

There was not much to offer in the way of food; we had only a few cooked bananas, which we shared. Masini Phillipe and the others were brought in and put in another part of the room. Masini and Tele both had wounds on their arms and wrists, from the ropes with which they had been bound. We shared our food and water with them too. They were then taken out and put in the proper prison building.

Later that morning we were informed that we were to be moved to another house; the Bongondza folk would be separated from us, so that they would be free to work at the hospital, but we would be prisoners in our house. We repacked our few goods and transferred to our new quarters.

The Bongondza party had a house about five hundred yards from ours; it was furnished even with curtains at the windows. They had guards to protect them, so they were told, from any anti-white demonstrations. The man I had led to Christ the first night was, we found out later, the chief of the military police, and it was he who chose our guards. The Bongondza house always had ex-Bongondza schoolboys, so they were happy with this arrangement.

Our house was almost opposite the ferry landing stage, the first house past the post office. There was very little furniture — a dining table and six chairs, with in another room a bedstead, the base of which was an open wove type made with vines, and in the next room nothing except an enormous wardrobe. This room had leading from it what we called the "sunroom", a long narrow room, four feet wide by twelve feet long; it trapped all the afternoon sun. There was also a filthy bathroom, in much the same state as in the first house.

Our hearts sank as we viewed our new quarters. The Administrator arranged for the bathroom to be cleaned, and water brought, so that helped somewhat, but on the matter of beds he could not help us. Later that day the teacher from Bodela, the Parrys' village, came with blankets for them, and they graciously shared them with us.

This first night the four Parrys slept on the bed frame, and Mary and I stretched out on the dining-room table. My, it was hard . . . Mary said the next day, she understood what the Psalmist meant when he said, "Thou tellest all my bones"; she did not realise she had so many till then! We slept there for two nights then we took out the shelves of the wardrobe in the inner room and placed them on the floor, and from then on slept on those. It was just as hard, but not quite so much in the public eye as we had been on the table.

After a few days a small trunk arrived from Bopepe with two blankets and two cushions, and some cutlery and plates; we at last felt civilised.

During this time Ian Sharpe and Ruby Gray had begun their work at the hospital. It was a fairly new hospital, very well-equipped with modern instruments and X-ray plant, and the operating theatre was equipped with all that a surgeon would need. The French doctor who had been in charge had been taken by the rebels to Stanleyville as Surgeon-in-Chief, and consequently there was nobody at Banalia hospital except an elderly Catholic nun and the Congolese staff. The sister was relieved of her work when the others arrived, though they did allow her two or three days to explain things to Ruby.

They were very busy at the hospital and were often called out at night too; most of the patients were rebel soldiers who had been wounded.

Just about this time the evangelist and his wife who had been so kind in feeding us were threatened if they came again, and I learned later that their house was burned to the ground. They had four young children and we felt it would not be fair to ask them to run risks for us, and sorrowfully we bade them farewell.

That was our food supply cut off. Now we wondered what the Lord was going to do to feed us. The answer came from an unexpected quarter.

It was 2.30 p.m. and we were sitting around the table. Mary was knitting, and the Parrys were playing Scrabble (Mary had packed it in her case). Suddenly the guards were changed, and we noticed they were all military policemen; usually only one in four was one. They brought their chairs *into* the house and sat facing us; the attitude was one of hostility, and they talked at us amongst themselves, as to how we were going to dance to their music. They kept looking out of the window and rubbing their hands together with obvious glee. Somebody was coming along the road that gave them much pleasure.

Mary said very quietly, "Go on playing your game as though nothing has happened, but at the same time pray." A crowd was gathering all round the house, and the tension became almost unbearable. A shout announced the arrival of three nuns and one priest, all barefoot, carrying their shoes and stockings in their hands. How pitiful they looked. They had been resting when the rebels arrived, and ordered them out on the road, minus shoes, and they forced them to walk on the stoniest parts, all the way to our house, almost a mile away.

They were pushed through into the room Mary and I had occupied, then the Simbas ordered us to remove our shoes and to follow the others. We were told to stand to attention, they then went out shutting the door behind them. We whispered together to find out what had happened, but none of us knew the answer.

The Simbas came back every ten minutes or so to taunt us, and to make sure we were still standing and not praying. The children were very good, and entered into the spirit of the situation without a murmur. The priest had a mild attack of angina and sat on the floor. The rebels were furious with him, and one kicked him. He remained, however, on the floor. One time, Dennis leaned against the wall and was not quick enough when the door reopened and he was struck across the face.

The sisters' house-boy brought rice and corned beef for them, but they were not hungry. They offered some to us, but neither were we hungry. We were not allowed any water.

As darkness fell at 6.30 the Simbas came in and took our lamp; we were left still standing in the dark. The Simbas on the verandah sang their songs of hate about the white people — they sang in Swahili. I was glad Mary could not understand the words, though all the Parrys did.

The children began to fidget at eight o'clock, and Nora asked permission for them to lie down, which was granted, and Nora was allowed to sit with them in their room. She was even allowed a light; we thanked the Lord for this respite for her.

How we prayed during the long hours of that night I do not know, except that two texts kept coming to my mind, "I will trust and not be afraid" (Isaiah 12:2), and the counterpart, "What time I am afraid, I will trust in Thee" (Psalm 56:3), and I know it was the latter I prayed more often than the former. I would say something like this: "Lord, I am afraid, therefore I am trusting in Thee to help us in this special hour of need."

How many times that prayer was prayed I do not know. The visits of the Simbas became more and more obnoxious; they said outrageous things, and threatened us with all kinds of torture.

One Simba came in with a pipe filled with hemp and, beginning with the sisters, tried to make us smoke it. The sisters refused, the priest accepted; he was a smoker normally, though not of hemp of course. Then they came to us. I was first. "Smoke this or we'll beat you," was the command, and I was given the courage to answer, "You will have to beat me then, for I'll not smoke." He then filled his mouth with smoke, and putting his nose against mine, blew the smoke over my face. It was quite simple to hold my breath. Then came Mary's turn, then Dennis and Nora; each time the same command, the same answer, and the same exhibition. He then came back to me and repeated the little act. He went out slamming the door behind him, and also the door leading to Nora's room. We breathed freely once again, and praised the Lord for His help at that stage, and asked for more help for the ensuing unknown hours.

The priest was then taken out to be with them, and they made him smoke the hemp for several hours, until eventually he kept vomiting and had to be put to bed – that is, laid out on the floor in Nora's room.

Around 12.30 a.m., with the exception of Mary, we were told to lie down on our so-called bed. We were placed three in a row – myself in the middle – with the eldest sister at our feet (which were filthy by this time), and we had to place our feet on her back; we tried to do it gently so as not to hurt her. Mary was taken to the bathroom and made to stand to attention by the side of the toilet; she had to stand there an hour, and was then brought back, and I took her place for another hour. During that hour a Simba crept back in the dark and grabbed me by my arms; I said if he did not leave me alone I would scream, so he apparently thought the better of his evil intentions and left me. After the hour, I was ordered to lie down again with Mary, and the three sisters and Dennis (who was brought back to our room) were made to stand to attention in the dark. This lasted for half an hour, and they were then told to lie down again. Dennis went back to Nora and the children, and the three sisters lay down with us.

At 4.30 a.m. the Simbas decided that Mary and I would dance to their music, and we were duly taken out to what had been the dining-room. We were still without shoes on our feet. By the feeble light of a palm-fat lamp we saw the Simbas sitting around, and one in particular dancing, a sensual dance usually reserved for the villages. He came to me to dance with him, but I refused to move; I guess my feet felt as though they had taken root just where they were. He threatened to beat me, but the Lord gave courage, and as I argued with him a Simba who had been in the shadows came into the light, and I recognised him as one who had arrested us at Bopepe. Apparently he was a senior military policeman, for he commanded this man to leave us alone, and threatened him with punishment if he tormented us any more. We were then ordered back to bed — once again we had cause to praise the Lord for His undertaking.

Never had a night seemed so long, but at last daylight came, and we were left alone.

My Bible was in Nora's room, and Mary's was in the little sun-room and the doors were firmly shut, but my *Daily Light* was with us. It was November 14th and I will quote it in full, as it was so topical, and gave us such comfort.

"Thou art my help and my deliverer; make no tarrying, O my God (Psalm 40: 17). The steps of a good man are ordered by the Lord: and he delighteth in his way. Though he fall, he shall not be utterly cast down: for the Lord upholdeth him with his hand (Psalm 37: 23 and 24). In the fear of the Lord is strong confidence: and his children shall have a place of refuge (Proverbs 14: 26). Who art thou, that thou shouldst be afraid of a man that shall die and of the son of man which shall be made as grass; and forgettest the Lord thy maker? (Isaiah 51: 12, 13). I am with thee to deliver thee (Jeremiah 1: 8). Be strong and of a good courage, fear not, nor be afraid of them; for the Lord thy God, he it is that doth go with thee; he will not fail thee, nor forsake thee (Deuteronomy 31: 6). I will sing of thy power; yea I will sing aloud of thy mercy in the morning: for thou hast been my defence and refuge in the day of trouble (Psalm 59: 16). Thou art my hiding-place; thou shalt preserve me from trouble; thou shalt compass me about with songs of deliverance (Psalm 32:7)."

These were the lovely promises which we could claim for ourselves; we shared them with the nuns. Mary translated them into French, and they too were visibly comforted.

Later that morning the door was thrust open and in came several senior rebels. The leader introduced himself as the District Commissioner. He was a short, stocky man, with an enormous black beard which seemed as though it hid half his face. He had on sun-glasses, of which one of the lenses was cracked, and he still had the price-tag stuck on the other one. He was supported by a large group of rebels, some soldiers, others presumably administrative staff, and right in the background was the Administrator.

The Commissioner was very voluble in bad French, and lectured us for half an hour. He said he was a Protestant and knew his Bible. He quoted how the Jews had been under Egyptian oppression, and how Moses was the God-appointed leader to lead them out, and then he went on to say that Lumumba was the God-appointed present-day Moses, that they, the Congolese, were like the Jews, and we, the whites, were the Egyptians. He reminded us of the fate of the Egyptians and said it would be our fate too. He then asked our nationalities. The Catholic sisters, who were Belgian, came in for his verbal abuse; he made fun of them, and almost spat upon the crucifix of one, then he vented his spite on Mary because she came from America. There was nothing we could do or say: what he had to say was so obviously propaganda, and so ridiculous that afterwards we could laugh at it all.

After he had finished, he marched out very pompously, attended by his retinue. The Administrator came back, and very quickly said that we were not to worry; it had been necessary to say all that or else lose face in front of his staff. We were grateful for that kind word, as we had felt pretty well beaten mentally. The sisters said the Commissioner looked like the devil, and from then on we referred to him as "Monsieur the Devil".

At midday the Administrator came back, and we were called into his presence. He was seated at the table, and we stood at attention in front of him, still in bare feet.

He too abused us verbally; we were so surprised after his words of kindness earlier on, but supposed it was for the same reason, the danger of losing face before his inferiors. He said we could put our shoes on and sit down again, and that we would not be tormented further unless something else happened nationally, when we would again be punished for the deeds of our relatives (i.e. the whites). We would, however, no longer have the freedom of the house, just the room we occupied and the bathroom, and our guard would be doubled.

We went back to our room grateful for even a small respite. Food was brought to us one hour later.

During the morning Nora Parry collapsed, and was taken to the hospital under Ian Sharpe's care; Dennis and the children went too. The Catholic priest was also sent there because of his heart condition, and he very kindly shared his food with the Parrys. Conditions there were terrible; nowhere to sleep, no water, no toilet facilities, and they were under constant supervision. The guards were very rude to them all. They had little peace whilst there. On the Sunday morning Dennis and Andrew were made to pick up leaves and rubbish in the grounds for two hours. They hit Dennis several times. On the Monday evening he and the children were sent back to our prison, leaving Nora alone without help. We sent several letters to the Administrator and eventually he allowed Nora to come back too. How glad we were to see her, though she had only been away three days. She looked so frail and tired, it was a joy to minister to her and make a fuss of her, the sisters vying with us to help.

Our days were spent reading and praying, playing Scrabble or just talking. We made our own amusement, taking it in turns to sit on one of the four chairs. I made a seat out of my case; it was rather low down, but at least it was not on the floor.

The house was situated right by the Administration post, and we would watch the Simbas each morning at seven o'clock roll-call. One morning we saw Phillipe Masini, his son Mbongo Samuel, and Tele Gaston, go marching by with the other prisoners; at least we knew they were still alive. Later we heard that Masini had been made foreman of the working party because of his exemplary conduct. We were so proud of him.

Often we would see the prisoners carrying another who had been so badly beaten he was unconscious, and frequently the man would die before roll-call was finished.

There was one man who was different from the other Simbas in that he had a military bearing and his clothes were always immaculate and in good condition as well. He would always be with the new recruits, and we rightly guessed he had been a sergeant-major in the National Army. He used to visit us in our prison. We thought he was crazy. He would march in, salute, and smartly stand to attention, and would then talk to us in disjointed sentences, using several languages, and laughing very heartily at the end of each sentence. Nothing he ever said made sense. Mary called him "Mr. Jingle" after Charles Dickens' character. We would watch for him each morning as he drilled his recruits. One evening when he came to see us he was slightly drunk; he laughed so heartily, throwing his head back to do so, that his hat fell off. His escort picked it up and put it back on his head for him, without so much as a smile.

On November 17th, we were informed that we were techni- cally free, and that Ian Sharpe and the others from Bongondza had been free all the time; Nora aptly described our freedom as the "freedom of compulsion". We were still strictly guarded, still not allowed to move in the house apart from our rooms. We discounted their idea of freedom, for we felt sure that one of the other folk would have been to see us if they had been allowed. Nora said that Ian had a guard wherever he went at the hospital, and Ruby too.

Looking out of the window we espied our tribal chief, Mulaba Fidele; he saw us and, permission being granted, he came to speak to us. He said they were trying hard for our release. He had come in every day with a different group of people to plead for us, and they had even signed a petition for us. His life was in danger as the rebels resented his interference on our behalf. He looked thin and tired, but his faith in the Lord was undimmed.

Towards the end of the third week a plane was heard overhead, and outside panic reigned. We wondered what it could mean, but were never enlightened. The rebels said that if it had bombed Banalia they would have shot us.

During all this time I pursued my usual Bible readings, and many were the promises of deliverance. One day in sharing these thoughts with Mary she said, "For you Margaret, but not for me; I think I am going to die here at Banalia." Another time she said that she felt the sentence of death was upon her, but felt I would be delivered. And a third time she said that of all places in Congo, she was glad it would be Banalia where she was going to die. No matter what I said to her, she was so sure she would die there.

Nora Parry had read the verse, "Now is your salvation nearer than when ye believed," and she said she felt that was the Lord's word to her heart to prepare her for death. In vain I remonstrated with her; I showed her the promises of deliverance I had received, and like Mary she said, "For you Margaret, but not for me." Her main concern was for the children. What would happen to them?

74

On November 23rd, a Monday, I was told that there would be a truck going past Banalia at 2 p.m. and that I was to get on it. In many ways I was fearful of returning to the village alone, as we were right on the main road, yet we felt sure that if I was released, the others would soon follow. Mary decided for me. I was to go back, put the house in order, and send provisions through, and a bicycle for her for when they released her, in case there was not a truck, as she could not face the prospect of walking all that way again.

So, armed with a list of things to send, and our dirty washing, I prepared to leave them. I called in on the Sharpes and told them I was going. Ian said he was going to Bongondza the next day to get further supplies, and that he would call in at Bopepe if they allowed him, to see if I was all right.

Not knowing what was going on in the world outside Banalia, I said that if the mercenaries came to rescue them, they were to remember me at Bopepe and to reserve a seat on the plane. Ian said very seriously, "Very well, Margaret, we'll meet either on the plane, or in Glory." Did he too have a premonition?

They had been well cared for, though always under guard. The children were allowed to play in the grounds and they lived a life as near normal as possible under the circumstances. In fact, when I went to say goodbye, they even had the table laid with a tablecloth and all the niceties of civilisation . . .

Goodbyes were said, and I went back to the others. Dennis came to the truck with me to carry my case; as we said goodbye he said, "We will be much in prayer for you there alone, and if we do not meet down here again, I will see you in Heaven."

A short word of prayer together, and I was off. As the ferry moved over the water, we waved to each other; I could see Mary very plainly at the window with the sisters and Nora for a long time.

As I stepped off the ferry I felt for the first time very alone,

75

even though I was surrounded by people. The promise I had received that morning was, "Whoso hearkeneth unto me shall dwell safely, and shall be quiet from fear of evil" (Proverbs 1: 33).

As I made my way back to Bopepe, and was putting things in order, the National Government were finalising plans for the rescue of the 1,200 white hostages in Stanleyville, of whom twenty-eight were from the Unevangelised Fields Mission.

On November 24th the plans were put into action, and by 3 p.m. Stanleyville was completely retaken by government troops. Most of the hostages were rescued, but over thirty-five lost their lives, including Hector McMillan of our mission, a Canadian and the father of six sons. He was normally stationed at Bongondza station with the Sharpes and Ruby Gray.

The loss of the city made it virtually a death-trap for any rebels caught there.

In the other direction another smaller city, Aketi, had, after much fighting, also fallen on November 24th, but the rebels there had not heard about Stanleyville.

On Wednesday, November 25th, these Simbas loaded their wounded on to a truck, and with a large number of armed Simbas, including two officers, they took the road to Stanleyville hospital.

They had to pass Bopepe and then Banalia, and it was when they arrived at Banalia that they first heard of the fall of Stanleyville and realised that their position was hopeless.

Earlier that week their "Prime Minister", Christophe Gbenye, had broadcast to his rebels that, in the event of an attack on Stanleyville, all white people were to be killed. The Simbas who had just arrived at Banalia were mad with rage, and demanded that the white prisoners be brought out. The time was 3.45 p.m.

Ian Sharpe was operating at the hospital, the patient was a wounded Simba. Audrey and the children, together with Ruby

Gray, were in their house. The Parry family, Mary Baker and the three sisters were in the prison-house, and the priest was in the hospital as a patient.

The rebels divided into three groups. The hospital group took a jeep and brought back both Ian and the priest, the Rev. Herman Bischoff, a Dutchman. They had shot the patient on the operating table, and the Congolese nurse who had been assisting the doctor.

The doctor and the priest were first back at the landing stage of the ferry; without further waiting, they were both killed and their bodies thrown into the Aruwimi River.

The guards at the other two places were overpowered and outnumbered; the missionaries and the children were then led out to the landing stage.

They were lined up in a row, and one by one called forward, and then killed; their bodies too, were thrown into the river. The time was 4 p.m.

"In death they were not divided."

"Be thou faithful unto death and I will give thee the crown of Life."

Thus they entered into the presence of the Lord to receive their crowns of Life.

Their bodies were never recovered, even though the Christians from Bopepe wanted to go and find them. Due to continual enemy activity in that area, the attempt had to be abandoned.

4

In the Jungle

THE truck was filled with Simbas going to a plantation for food. I was wedged into the cabin between two of them. The door on the passenger side was tied shut with wire, the ignition key was missing, and the truck was started by manipulating two wires — I was to see this hundreds of times in later weeks, but this was my first time in a rebel-controlled vehicle.

The villages were still fairly well populated, and as we neared the chief's village we heard singing. As we passed it we noticed it was filled with people singing and dancing. We had to slow down, for the crowds spilled over on to the roads; several people recognised me, and promptly left the dancing and followed us to Bopepe.

My welcome back was very heart-warming, and it was lovely to see the dear ones again. The Simbas inspected our house, and asked me to report if anything had been taken then, demanding food to be ready against their return next day, left us. Then it was that the villagers really gathered round. Some wept, some danced, all demanded news of the others at Banalia.

Mary's dog came bounding towards me, and my black cat rubbed contentedly against my legs. I made the inevitable cup of tea, but it was almost impossible to drink it due to the constant stream of visitors. My, but it was grand to be home again!

We talked about sending a bicycle and escort to Banalia for Mary (this was still Monday, November 23rd).

Bo Martin arranged with his wife that I should eat there that evening, which left me free to clean the house and generally

78

take a good look at the situation in which we found ourselves.

In the evening the young girl who used to sleep with us before we were arrested came again, and I moved her bed into my room and by ten o'clock we were in bed. I could not sleep very much, so at midnight got up and washed my hair. Eventually at 2.30 a.m. I went back to bed and slept soundly until 5.30.

The day began normally, though there was a feeling of tension. The house-boy came, and was effectively employed with the enormous amount of washing brought back from Banalia. I went down to the dispensary and maternity and cleaned right through and prepared it all to be reopened the next day. Several mothers came to show me their babies, and we talked of many things. Lunch over, I felt free to sort out some of the things requested by the Banalia folk, and packed them into cartons convenient for carrying.

At 3 p.m. all was quiet, unnaturally so. I was in Bo Martin's house, when two of the schoolteachers came over and spoke to Bo in the tribal tongue — they were very excited and at the same time apprehensive. Bo turned to me and said, "Stanleyville has fallen, and the National Army are coming this way, you must go to the forest with the women." I argued, but he insisted that as a woman I had no place in war, and as a white woman it placed them all in danger. He became cross with me because I hesitated, and said that the safety of the village depended upon my going with the women and children to the forest. He had hardly done speaking when the drums were heard from the chief's village — he too was ordering all women and children to the forest, and all men to defend their villages. A few minutes later, a special runner came in from the chief's village to order me immediately into the forest with the others.

I felt sick. Almost mechanically I took the washing off the line, repacked my case, and collected a small overnight bag and a lantern. My thoughts were racing. What about the friends in Stanleyville? What about friends at Banalia, Aketi, and Bafwasende? What was happening to them? I could only whisper, "Dear Lord, I don't understand, but I'm trusting you to take care of the situation."

We have much to learn from our Congolese women, not least how to walk through the forest with a load on the back without tripping, and at an incredible speed. I was so ashamed; there was I, a weak, pampered white woman, unable to carry my suitcase more than a few yards without puffing and panting and changing hands, when one of the women carrying a load larger than herself, plus a baby on her hip, swung my case up on top of her load almost without a pause in her pace, and then went on as quickly as ever!

The hideout had been prepared weeks before, and was three miles (five kilometres) into the forest. We had to cross a fairly large river over a fallen tree trunk. I wanted to close my eyes but dared not do so. They scrambled over trees, under trees, through mud and water, and I straggled along behind, doing my best to keep up with them and consequently tripping, catching my clothes in the bushes and stubbing my toes.

Practically exhausted, I arrived at our destination to find the women busy preparing food; others were cutting wood for beds, others had gone for water. Everybody knew what to do and how to do it. Never had I felt so white as on that day! The confusion was something to behold, yet in the midst of it sat a young mother serenely feeding her baby as though all were quiet. Even the little three-and four-year-olds were occupied in gathering sticks for the fire.

We were all apprehensive, and were glad when at ten o'clock two of the men came through to give us the radio report and to stay the night.

Thirty-seven white people killed in Stanleyville! I was in torment wondering if any of our friends were included. Nobody knew. They had listened to names, but foreign names are not easy for them to remember. Our folks at Aketi had been rescued, for the radio said as much. None of us slept that night; we read and prayed, and talked and wondered.

Happily for us it was not the rainy season, and though very cold at night, at least it was dry. The day dawned at last, November 25th.

The families split up for chores. Some went for water, some for firewood, and others cooked, and the children helped cut back the forest a little more to make it lighter.

During the afternoon hours I sat with Mary's dog at my feet, trying to pray but with such uneasiness of spirit that there seemed to be no release from strain.

Around four o'clock, the dog suddenly sat up, ears pricked forward, and whined and whined. We thought there must be a wild animal in the vicinity, and several called the dog to go with them to investigate, but he stayed with me, crying for about half an hour, then with a big sigh lay down again at my feet. I tried to comfort him, but was so uneasy myself I do not think I helped him at all. Looking back later, I realised it was at that time our friends in Banalia were being hastened into the Kingdom of God.

The evening was spent reading and praying, and when the men came through at ten o'clock with the radio news, there was nothing outstanding to report. We fully expected the National Army to be along in a day or two. Bo's wife said she thought we would be in the forest a week; I did not feel as though I could stand the strain for so long. The Lord had much to teach me in the ensuing days!

I slept a little that night, and was just about washed next morning when Paul Ponea, our young school director came and sat by me, and very quietly told me to pack my things quickly; I was to be moved. Something in his eyes told me to obey and not to quibble. In a few minutes I was saying my goodbyes to the women, many of whom wept, whilst others turned their backs in sorrow. Paul had talked to them in the tribal language, and asked them not to demonstrate about what they had heard until I was told, which would be a little later.

Once again that awful feeling of sickness through apprehension was present, and yet I dared not ask why I alone was being moved. After ten minutes' travel, Paul turned round and just said, "Oh, Mademoiselle!" in such a way I knew something had gone wrong. He looked absolutely broken. I asked him to tell me what was the matter, but he could not, at that time, speak, for emotion.

My *Daily Light* reading that morning had said, "Fear not . . . thou art Mine" – it was hard not to fear in the face of the unknown.

After about a mile we met two of the teachers, who were out of breath and kept looking at me as they spoke in rapid-fire tribal language. They passed us, and Paul called me to him. "Mademoiselle Margarita, I do not know how to tell you, but all the white people at Banalia were killed yesterday afternoon. When we first heard, we sent a runner in to find out if it was true and he has come back and alas, it is true. They are all with the Lord. Now they are coming to find you to kill you, so Bo sent me ahead to fetch you and we will meet him further along and he will hide you away alone until the National Army comes."

I was stunned. I believe I asked the one word question, "All?" And Paul answered so gently and with such obvious sorrow, "Yes, all of them, Mary included." I scarcely know how I followed him along. Inside, I was numb.

We met Bo. He hugged me. "Thank God you are still alive. Oh Margarita, my heart is broken! – but come, there is no time for sorrow, you must be hidden because they are looking for you."

Up to this time Mary's dog had been with me, and it was decreed he must go back to the women, and leave me alone.

We walked on in silence through the forest. I do not know how I did it, but somehow we arrived at a tiny clearing. Bo had been to the house and brought along a lounge chair for me. He went off somewhere and came back with a pineapple, and I realised it was midday and I was thirsty. Bo had to leave me there for several hours whilst he saw to other things in the village, but promised to be back before nightfall.

My thoughts were in a whirl. Why? Why? Why? And then I would think of them all in Glory with the Father, and was glad for them. I prayed for courage to face a violent death as a true believer, and was even able later to praise Him for taking them all to be with Himself. As Geoffrey Bull puts it so beautifully in his book *God Holds the Key*, "Departure is really only a transfer from one sphere of service to another, by the Master Who knows what He is doing and never errs."

Later that night, with Bo, we shared *Daily Light*. We read: "The Lord hath anointed me to preach good tidings to the meek; he hath sent me to bind up the broken-hearted, to comfort all that mourn ... to give unto them the oil of joy for mourning, the garment of praise for the spirit of heaviness" (Isaiah 61: 1 and 3).

Bo lit a fire, and having brought himself a deck chair, we settled down for the night. Our cover for the night was a tiny leaf roof about eight feet by five feet, supported on four poles; there were no walls.

"In everything give thanks," says the Word of God, so I thanked Him for the dry season and a roof over our heads.

Occasionally I would see Bo wipe away his tears, and wished I too could find relief in them, but somehow they would not come. I was probably still in a state of shock.

Bo wanted to go to Banalia to recover the bodies from the river and then bring them back to Bopepe for burial by the Church. He took fifteen blankets from the hospital and was preparing his bicycle to go, when the village elders forbade him as it was too dangerous with the Simbas still there, especially so whilst they were out hunting for me. Poor Bo, his loyalties were divided, but I feel that he probably would have lost his life on such a mission, for the Simbas who were there then were so anti-white they would not waste sympathy on a pastor looking for the bodies of his white friends.

We stayed in the hideout for several days, and one by one the women came to visit me; they would weep, holding on to me, and I feel that though this was their custom, they were genuine in their grief and in their concern for me. One woman, one of our few deaconesses, came and wept long and loudly at my feet; when I tried to comfort her by reminding her that our friends were with the Lord and would not want us to grieve, she put her thoughts very succinctly and said, "But I'm not weeping for them, I'm weeping for us that are left behind." For us that are left behind – yes, that was us. It then dawned upon me that, of those I had been with in Banalia, I alone was left.

One evening, four or five days after the massacre, Bo said he was going to transfer me to the village as he felt sure the National Army would be along any time. It was strange to be in the almost deserted village, and to see the men with whom we were associated in our work. As they brought me some food many of them broke down and wept. That evening, a runner came through bringing news from Banalia and the names of all who had died. It was all too true, there were no survivors.

That night Bo put a folding bed for me in one of his outhouses, and he slept on guard, as he was not awfully sure about the safety of the village. The next day I had to go back into the forest to a place that he and his brother had made, which was like the previous place only larger. Bo brought one or two oddments from the house and it was comparatively comfortable.

I stayed there for a further three weeks, during which time the Simbas came to the village several times demanding me, and then they added Bo to the list, so that he had to stay with me in hiding too. He was so kind, going out of his way to find things for my added comfort.

During this time I would spend the better part of every day just reading my Bible and praying. The Psalms were a great source of comfort, and also the books of Jeremiah and Isaiah. In thinking through my amazing deliverance from Banalia, I felt sure that it was not just accidental nor coincidental. My work was not finished, whereas my colleagues had completed theirs and had heard the "Well done—enter thou into the Presence of thy Lord." The more I thought about this the more convinced I was that the Lord would have me continue my work in the Congo, so then and there, in the solitude of the African jungle, with only the insects and trees as my witnesses, I rededicated my life afresh to the Lord, to go or stay, to die or live in His service. This conviction has never left me.

On November 30th, the Africans heard planes in the distance, and then later, bombs; on investigation it was found that they were bombing Banalia. Every day for a week the planes came. They did not do much damage, but they did frighten the people and the Simbas into the forest. On Tuesday, December 8th, a plane came very low over Bopepe, and flew over the village twice. One or two said they saw a man with binoculars, it may have been true, but I was in the forest and to my chagrin was unable to signal to the plane. I had made a note in my Bible, "Still looking to the Lord to effect *His* deliverance" (Ezekiel 34: 11 and 12).

The Simbas in the locality were furious, and said I had called the plane to find me and to bomb them. Efforts were renewed to find us in order to kill us.

One evening the following week, everyone was in great excitement: the National Army had said they would come to Banalia that day. The Africans had heard gun-fire and bombs, and expected them along our road, but one bomb had destroyed the ferry and there was no way across. I heard later it was the mercenaries who had come; they only stayed one night and then went on to rescue the white people elsewhere. There were many Simbas wounded and they came to Bopepe for treatment, but the men were afraid to let me go to them, so did not tell me until after they had left.

The next night one of the men heard on his radio the National Army report that all white people at Banalia had been killed and there were no survivors. *They did not know I was alive!*

All hopes of being rescued were dashed to the ground, and I suddenly felt very alone, caught up in a situation beyond my mortal comprehension.

My reading that day was in Micah, and as I read chapter 7, I felt rebuked for my lack of faith. Verses 7–9 read, "Therefore will I look unto the Lord, I will wait for the God of my salvation, My God will hear me. Rejoice not against me, O mine enemy; when I fall, I shall arise, when I sit in darkness, the Lord shall be a light unto me . . . He will bring me forth to the light, and I shall behold His righteousness."

The following day we had rain; the skies just opened and it was a deluge, which does happen during the dry season from time to time. It matched my mood. It seemed to put the final touch to everything for me. I had been glad for the dry weather as I knew the road from Stanleyville to Banalia was bad in *fine* weather, and had it rained it would have been very difficult for the army to get through safely. Now they had been and gone, and it did not seem to matter any more how much it rained. We were soaked, but Bo lit a fire as soon as it became dark and we were able to dry out.

My thoughts would wander to home; it was almost Christmas, there would be carols, and trees lit up. There would be the happy exchange of presents, the shops would be filled with the excited and desperate last minute shoppers, and how I longed to be in with it. At times it was almost unbearable to think about it.

It dawned upon me that once I was reported dead, there would not be any prayer support from anybody. I was appalled and asked the Lord then and there to get it across somehow to somebody, that I was not dead, and to burden them to pray. I prayed this prayer at least once a day until the middle of the following March, when I thought I knew folks at home knew I was alive. How the Lord so wonderfully answered that prayer

I was not to know until my eventual return home six months later.

By December 19th, the Simbas began to be more insistent about my coming out of the forest, and threatened war with the village. On Sunday the 20th they came and filled the village. Bo took me from our hiding place and hid me in thick, dark, damp jungle, with instructions not to move. I heard the Simbas searching in the undergrowth not very far away. Sometime during the day, Bo crept back to me and without saying a word gave me some bananas to eat. We could hear the Simbas arguing in the village. I thought of all the promises which the Lord had made to me when I was first called to Congo, one being the well-known verse from Joshua 1, "Be not afraid, neither be thou dismayed, for the Lord thy God is with thee whithersoever thou goest." I remember whispering, "Yes, Lord, I believe You are with me but I'm both afraid and dismayed at the moment." It did not quite make sense to me; had I escaped the massacre at Banalia in order to die like a hunted animal in the forest? My thoughts went back to the last leaders' conference we had held, and Bob McAllister preaching on "Not my will but Thine". As I thought about this I remembered that the Lord had asked that the cup might pass from Him, nevertheless ... Had I reached the place where I could say, "Nevertheless, not my will but Thine"? If that was the Lord's will for my life, then the responsibility was His, and He *had* promised to be with me. He brought great peace to my heart as I began to cease to worry and leave the consequences to the Lord.

It was not much longer after this that Bo came back with his son, Stetefano, an eleven-year-old, and to him was given the job of guarding me and leading me back to our hideout when evening fell. The boy stayed with us at night. As we shared our time of prayer together, Bo turned again to *Daily Light* for the evening portion, December 20th: "With God all things are possible" ... "have I no power to deliver?" ... "Lord it is nothing with Thee to help, whether with many or with them that have no power". This was the last time we read that little book together.

At the first sign of dawn we were up, and after a short word of prayer for guidance we had struck camp and were moving to another place.

We struggled through thick jungle, waded down a river and then back into the jungle. Bo made a tiny clearing, and whilst he and the boy went back for the rest of the things I cooked some rice on the primus-stove we had brought with us. During the day, Bo cut down small bamboo branches and some small trees to make us another roof before night came.

Suddenly at 3.30 p.m. we heard shooting and men yelling "Simba! Simba!" We heard them running down the pathway and into the forest to where the village women had their camp. The drums beat the war-cry. Bo grabbed his briefcase, I a small hand-grip, and Stetefano had something, but I cannot remember what it was. Bo signalled to me to follow, and we plunged into the thick undergrowth, back through the river, on and on through thick jungle. We heard a lot of shooting and women screaming, the Simbas called out to me several times to give myself up, but Bo told me to be quiet and not move.

We lay low until nightfall, when Bo led us out into somebody's maize garden where we met with some men from another village who had come to defend Bopepe. They led us to the women's camp, but there were no women, only men engaged in an argument, who, when they saw Bo, cheered and clapped.

They hid me behind a little leaf wall, the other side of which was a wounded Simba, and the men were debating whether or not to kill him. Nobody had been killed from the village, but Bo's eldest brother's wife, Ruta, had been taken prisoner by the Simbas.

Bo heard both sides of the argument. The Simba, a young man of twenty, an adjutant, had been detailed to wreck Bopepe village but not to kill, only to frighten the villagers. He had been afraid to do this, but had been threatened by his senior officers with beating and demotion if he failed in the attempt. He was wounded, and caught by the men of the village and brought to trial. Most of them wanted to kill him then and there, whilst others argued against, and it was this argument we had heard as we approached.

Bo explained that as Christians, we had an example to give. We were here to build up the Church and glorify the Lord, not to kill our enemies. If we were really Christian we would forgive them.

He finally had his way, and he was going to let the man go back to the Simbas, but the other men disagreed, and all except one, Bo's brother, walked off and left him. The Simba's rifle was taken from him and hidden. His wounds were washed, he was untied, and we formed a small procession back to the village, the Simba in front, Bo's brother, Bo and myself. It was a beautiful night, with a full moon; it seemed hard to believe that so much beauty could be present when there was so much ugliness around us.

We reached the river. The Simba bathed, and was then put on the last short path to the village and let free.

Bo's brother left us, and Bo, to my astonished eyes, dived into an enormous thick chunk of jungle with instructions for me to follow. What a night! It was now 11.30 p.m. We fell over logs, were scratched by bushes, lost I do not know how many times, and finally by 3 a.m. we had arrived at the back of one of the Bopepe houses. It had taken three and a half hours to traverse half a mile of jungle!

The Simbas were still in the village. We could hear them laughing and talking. We found out later that they had been systematically looting every house prior to burning them down.

Bo's plan was to enter the jungle on the other side of the main road; our problem was to cross the main road in bright moonlight, as they had sentries placed all along the road.

In that awful fight through the thick undergrowth, I had lost my hand-grip and Bo his briefcase. We had nothing but what we had on, and no Bible either!

At 4 a.m. the road seemed quiet enough for us to cross, and Bo gave me my instructions, to jump down into the road then run along in the shadow on the right for about fifty yards, then cross to a small pathway on the left. That was what we did. It was a sad sight to see Bo a fugitive from his own people in his own village.

We successfully crossed over, and quickly made our way deep into the jungle on the other side. All I could think of at that time was how thirsty I was, as we had not had a thing since 8 a.m. the previous day. We found somebody's sugar-cane and Bo cut it and we both ate it gratefully.

We then lay down on the ground to wait for daylight. I cannot remember what my thoughts were, I was too exhausted.

By daylight we were up again and on our way. In Congo the dew is very heavy, and it was not long before we were both soaking wet; my wet dress clinging to my legs did not help the tramp through the forest. Sometime during the night I had broken my sandal strap and was having difficulty in keeping it on.

The trail led through thick black mud, and at times we were ankle-deep in it. To say we looked a sorry sight would be an understatement. I had to slow down my pace, my sandal was not helping and I had developed a blister. My legs were all scratched and wading through mud made them sting. Bo was very patient with me, and we stopped several times for a breather, and several times he carried me over the muddy patches.

We found a pineapple patch and helped ourselves; never has pineapple tasted so good.

Finally at 9 a.m. we met up with a Christian family, my dispensary gardener and his wife! They gave us rice and peanuts, and hot water with which to wash. They even fixed a little lean-to for us to rest in before going any further. We gratefully lay down to rest, but it was cold and the ground was hard, and the emotional strain had been such, it was impossible to relax.

We stayed the night, but next morning we heard that the Simbas had killed two members of a Bopepe family, and that every house was burnt to the ground. They were beginning to burn down the next village and our school director, Ponea Paul, was being led about with a rope around his neck to find me.

I decided I must give myself up, and together we prayed that the Lord's will be done.

The gardener gave me two pieces of paper and a pen, and I wrote a farewell letter to my parents and to the General Director of the Mission in England. I asked the gardener to give them to the National Army when and if they came through.

This was Wednesday, December 22nd; it took us a further twenty-four hours to find our way out again, due to my slowness in walking, as my feet and legs were now infected and beginning to swell. It rained several times, and we were absolutely drenched through each time. There was no shelter, and when it rains in the dry season, the skies just open freely.

I was so weary, and asked the Lord for at least a roof over our heads for my (as I thought) last night on earth. We found a small shelter and Bo made a fire and we were able to dry out. Bo had a box of matches wrapped in a leaf in his pocket, and they had kept dry!

What was left of the night (it was 2 a.m.) I spent mostly praying for all my loved ones at home.

Morning came, and this time we found we were fairly near the Simba camp. We found a young man to lead me in, and I sadly took my leave of Bo.

Strange, but all fear of death had left me, and I found myself looking forward to meeting the Lord and the others who had been killed a month before.

It was Christmas Eve, 1964. I quoted Psalm 23 to myself as I walked along behind my guide. I remember asking the Lord to let it be a quick death with a bullet, and to help me to die as a true believer.

At 9.30 a.m. we reached the village of Bopando, the chief's village, three miles from Bopepe on the way to Banalia, where the Simbas had their headquarters. Thankfully I took the proffered chair a villager gave me whilst they went to call the Major.

5

Nurse-Prisoner of the Rebel Army

WHILST I was waiting for the rebels to come for me, the villagers crowded round; they were not really hostile, but neither were they friendly. One man had on a pair of my shoes; I realised with astonishment that I had last seen them in my bedroom a month before. He saw me looking at them, and volunteered the information I already knew: "They were in your house, and fit me nicely. We have taken all your things away." I asked what was my crime, and he pointed first to his skin and then to mine. "You are white and a friend of the American capitalists."

After a short while we heard a car; my escort had arrived, two rebel officers. They were very rude to me, and pushed me into the car. We did not go far, but as it was raining it was important that the rebels did not get wet and thereby lose the power of the magic on their bodies. I was already soaking wet so it did not matter to me any more.

The car had belonged originally to the French doctor who had been at Banalia, and in it were many mementoes of him, not least the chemistry note-book of his schoolgirl daughter. Somehow seeing this book comforted me.

Arriving at the main house they occupied, I was pushed into a large room and somebody was despatched to call the senior Major. I took stock of my surroundings. The verandah was full of dancing, chanting women, many of whom I recognised as former patients of Bopepe. They did not give any sign of recognition.

In the room were many Simbas, several of whom had rifles

and the rest had spears. It was these latter who danced round and round me, brandishing their spears and thrusting them almost into my face. Their dancing was very insinuating and revolting, though I dared not show my feelings. One Simba, who was particularly repulsive in his actions, came to me and said he was going to have the greatest pleasure in thrusting his spear through my face. Another came with a long, thin hunting knife and said he had been delegated to cut my throat that afternoon.

"You are a Protestant missionary, aren't you? Well then, you will not mind dying as you believe you will go to heaven." I answered in the affirmative, and added that I hoped he too had the same assurance for himself. He then asked if I was afraid to die, and when I said I was not, he looked at me for a long time and then slowly said that he really believed me.

This ludicrous situation lasted about an hour, then we heard orders being shouted, and the door behind me opened to admit the short stocky figure of the Major followed by his usual retinue. I must have cut a sorry figure, uncombed for four days, dirty, dress wet and torn, hair wet and hanging lankily round my ears, legs swollen from infection and sandals almost off my feet!

His first reaction was to order a chair for me, and when I was seated he turned to me for interrogation. He was of my height, that is just over five feet; middle-aged, with a kindly face, and clean shaven. He wore a leopard-skin, sleeveless jacket, and khaki shorts; round his neck, together with the numerous medicine charms, was a human thumb!

"Are you the white woman from Bopepe? Where have you been? How did you get here?" I answered that I was the white woman, and that I had given myself up in order to prevent further bloodshed and reprisals being taken on the population. I added, "If you want to kill me go ahead, but please leave my friends alone." To my surprise he said, "You are not going to die, we want you to work," and then turned on his heel and walked out leaving me quite deflated and wondering just what was ahead. I could only pray silently, asking for grace to meet this next phase of my life.

One of the officers, a lieutenant, stayed behind, and he gave orders for the Simbas to leave me alone, and for somebody to find food for me. Lieutenant Dieu-Donné was very friendly and even sympathetic, and drawing a chair up to the table motioned for me to sit across from him.

He began to interrogate me about my life before and after my arrival in Congo. He volunteered the information that he was a Catholic, but had been four years in the U.F.M. primary school at our station of Ekoko, and that he had been a bank clerk in Stanleyville.

Everything I said was taken down to be used in their statement either for or against me.

Halfway through, the door reopened and they brought in a woman; he asked me to turn round to see if I knew her. Knew her! She was my faithful helper in the maternity – Mama Ruta we all called her, the wife of the brother of Bo who had released the wounded Simba.

Satisfied that I knew her and probably confirmed her word to them, she was taken out again with her guard. I was disturbed at seeing Mama Ruta under such conditions and asked why she was there. They replied that they were holding her. Primarily until I gave myself up, and secondarily, the villagers had taken a rifle of the Simbas and until this was returned, she would remain a prisoner.

A little later a plate of pineapple was brought in and proceedings stopped whilst I ate, obviously hungrily, as the officer remarked on how hungry I was! The interrogation continued, and was again interrupted when a plate of rice and mushrooms came, with a spoon and a mug of water.

When the interrogation was finished, I was sent to the prison part of the village. Mama Ruta had to prepare hot water for me to wash, and they gave me soap. I was grateful for this, though I wished I had a towel. I put my dirty clothes on again, but they sent a comb and I felt better able to face my captors.

My legs and feet were the cause of much concern, and a "nurse" was sent to treat them.

I sat with Mama Ruta. She lived in a filthy hovel, and slept on boards. For some time we did not speak as there were many who were standing around, but when we were alone, we had much to say. She, poor dear, was almost sick with worry, for they kept telling her that her husband was dead. Also she asked me where Bo had hidden the rifle. Great was her surprise when I told her that it was her husband who had hidden it, and if he were dead . . . !

We discussed the fact that this was indeed Christmas Eve and we laughed at the incongruity of the situation. Somehow I dared not let my thoughts dwell too much on what was happening at home: carols, presents, parties, and all the things with which we keep Christmas there.

I had hoped to be home by then, but for some reason the Lord saw fit to allow me to share in the meanness and poverty of that first Christmas long ago, when the Babe of Bethlehem was born in a stable. As I looked around me, I wondered if there was any comparison. The chickens were scratching everywhere, half-starved dogs moped about in the dirt, the raucous voices of men who had been drinking grated on our ears, and I thought that it was under similar conditions that Joseph had led Mary to the stable, when there was no room in the inn. Pictures depict the stable as being clean and wholesome, but I doubt if it was.

"In everything give thanks" — the thought came back, and I was able to thank the Lord for sending His Son into the world in order that the world might be saved, and that He was allowing me, in some small way, the privilege of sharing in the fellowship of His sufferings.

More food was prepared for me by Mama Ruta, but she herself did not eat. The others around said she had not touched food for days. I am afraid I ate with a good appetite.

Margaret Hayes

Mary Baker, with her dog

Ruby Gray

Pastor Bo Marti
on the left, with
his brother Asa
and a Pigmy
convert

Bopepe Church

The dispensary at Banjwadi

Bongondza Hospital and Dispensary

The Parry family. Hazel and Stephen, in the centre, were in England at the time of the uprising, and so escaped massacre

Dr. Ian Sharpe with his wife Audrey and the children, Jillian, Alison and Andrew

The ferry landing-stage at Banalia, the scene of the November massacre

A group of Simba soldiers

The Sisters with the parrot that spoke in five languages

At the convent at Buta on Easter Sunday, 1965. Madame Le Gros, in the centre, has her hands on Ann's shoulders; Chantal is on the left

= F E U I L L E D E R O U T E =

Suite au Télégramme n° 579/CAB/PRES/64 du Président
de la République Populaire du Congo, Monsieur, Madame, Mademoiselle;
MARGARET Hayes

Accompagné de ....

Est (sont) autorisé de se rendre de Banalia à BOPEPE

Motif Reprendre ses activités

Fait à Banalia, le 23 novembre 1964;-

BOU... ...LAMBERT
ADMINISTRATEUR TERRITORIAL
CHEF DE TERRITOIRE

N.B : La présente donne accès libre aux Intéressés

Margaret Hayes' road pass, giving her permission to go back to take up her
work in Bopepe. It was issued at Banalia on November 23rd, 1964. Pastor Bo
Martin found it much later in the forest

A Nationalist Army convoy on the road to Banalia

The queue of refugees at Stanleyville, waiting to be repatriated

The rain cleared, and the women I had seen when I first arrived began to dance in the open. It was fairly near, so I hobbled over to see if I could speak to any of them. One of them was the young wife of one of our evangelists. She saw me looking, and turned her head away. Nobody would acknowledge me, so I sadly made my way back to Mama Ruta.

It was 5 p.m. before the Simbas let the women go back to their villages, and then it was that one of them, the "President of the political group" in her village, came and asked me to go to see the women as they had been afraid of the Simbas before. As I neared them, the group suddenly broke up and they all came running to me and hugged me. Many wept openly at my plight, they were all concerned at how thin I was. More than anything, I valued their friendship in a world which had suddenly seemed unfriendly. It was a lovely Christmas present for me, to be reinstated in their affections, though I do not think they had ever been really against me.

The Major came back. I could hear him calling to first one and then another of the officers to go to him. More food was given me, and afterwards it was my turn to go in to him. Mama Ruta took my hand and whispered that she would pray for me.

I was ushered into a small bedroom in a mud-walled house. It was dark and there were two palm-oil makeshift lamps burning. The Major was sitting on the edge of the bed in his underpants; by his side was his wife of the moment, a young arrogant girl. On the floor in front of them was their supper, rice and fish. They ate with their fingers and spat the bones on the floor all around.

A chair was given me, and I sat and watched him eat, and also interview various others and hear complaints. He finally bellowed for Lieutenant Dieu-Donné to come in with his report about me. I was asked to state my case again, and after every few sentences he would yell "Liar" at me, until finally I said it was not much point in telling him anything as he did not believe me, therefore I would not say any more. He looked quite astounded and quietened down considerably. He asked where Bo had gone, and asked me if I knew that they had killed eight people of Bopepe—all men. I felt sick with grief and worry as he did not seem to know who they were. Later a friendly Simba said it was only two dead.

His wife then locked the door from the inside. I began to feel apprehensive. He pointed to the bed, and said very gently, "Do not be afraid, I will not touch you. Go right over to the other side of the bed, and my wife will sleep in the middle. Do not be afraid, I will protect you." His wife then gave me a pillow which had come from Mary's bed, and one of her sheets too! I clambered over the bed as best I could, as my legs were very painful, and wrapping myself in Mary's sheet, lay down.

As I prayed for protection for the night and grace to go through whatever was ahead of me, I also had time to thank the Lord for a bed and a roof over my head. I fell asleep as soon as I had finished praying and slept soundly all night. I awakened at 7.30 a.m. to find I was alone in the room, and judging by the noise outside the day's activities were well in hand.

When I opened the tiny window, things became clear to my vision which the night before had been in obscurity. As I glanced round the room, there at the foot of the bed was the premature baby basket which I had kept in the house at Bopepe and it was filled with my clothes! Hanging on the wall were some more. On a chair by the bed was the large mirror from our bathroom. I studied the bed; the other pillows were our cushions, and the blanket the Major had used was Mary's.

As I tried to take in all this the Major's wife came in and said I was wanted outside. There was no need to dress—I had not undressed. As I put my feet on the ground, I found they were too swollen to wear my sandals, and the infection was really making itself felt. I could barely walk. The Major was quite sorry for me, and ordered the "nurse" to treat me.

Mama Ruta was there. She said they had told her that the village had given up the rifle they had hidden, and she was

free, but she would have to stay and look after the Mademoiselle. I was horrified and begged them to let her go. About
4 p.m. they consented.

Christmas Day! "Peace on earth and goodwill towards men"
—and there I sat in the middle of a group of blood-thirsty
Simbas! The Lord gave peace even in this situation, and yes,
the goodwill was there too. Lieutenant Dieu-Donné brought
out an accordion; it had come from our station at Bunga and
had belonged originally to Miss Viola Walker, a Canadian
veteran missionary of our mission. He asked me to name some
carols, and for the space of an hour and a half played "Silent
Night", "Noel", and "Hark the Herald angels sing", over and
over again.

Strange, this boy had been in Yugoslavia and Moscow for
military training, yet though subsequently he told me that
religion was the opiate of the people, he played the carols on
Christmas Day to comfort the heart of a lonely Protestant
missionary prisoner!

My Christmas dinner was not turkey but elephant meat; not
roast potatoes but boiled rice. They gave me enormous helpings
and were upset when I found it too much to manage.

Lieutenant Dieu-Donné asked if I had a case or anything
hidden in the forest which I could bring out so that I would
have something else to wear. Bo had told me where he had
hidden my suitcase, but it did not seem right to tell the rebels
just where, as they would once again be on Bopepe property.

Dieu-Donné said he personally would take me to find it, and
protect me at the same time, but not on Christmas Day, the
following Monday.

The men became drunk, and Mama Ruta left me. Several
women of the various villages came in and also some of the
village elders who had, in the past, been to Bopepe for treatment. It was good to see them, but there was a reserve about
what they said to me. One man started to say something about
Paul Ponea and another man immediately held his hand over

his mouth. They wanted me to believe Paul was dead, and I think this man was trying to reassure me to the contrary.

Many of the women were wearing my clothes; my uniforms had been cut in half to make blouses and underskirts; one woman even wore the top of a nylon nightie of mine!

About the third day, to my amazed astonishment, the Major came out in a pair of shorts made out of nursery material with which I made things for the maternity. It was in two colours, pink with little pale blue puppies with yellow bows, or pale blue with pink puppies with yellow bows. On this occasion he wore pink with blue puppies. He was so proud of them, he even took roll call in them! The other officers were jealous, and he had to give them some material too. So there they were, some in pink, some in blue, and some in patch-work made from the odds and ends!

Another officer carried his spare bullets in one of my bright green cushion covers. Everywhere he went he took it with him. Happily we were not engaged in any fighting else he would have had a hard time reloading his rifle in a hurry.

One boy, who could not have been more than seventeen years of age, turned up one day wearing three of my hair curlers on his wrist, pink and blue they were, and round his neck the polythene tubing and glass connections of a blood-transfusion set. On his hat, which was cowboy style, he had two of our bright orange nylon pot-scourers. He had on a pair of surgical gloves and to cap everything, a very worn-out pair of galoshes!

He went on parade dressed thus, but nobody took any special notice.

One day the Major turned up in Ruby Gray's full length, pale blue candlewick housecoat. He was the envy of the other men. Later that same day, he took it off, and came out in Mary Baker's pink bathrobe. He wore it back to front until somebody pointed out to him the buttons should be down the front.

On another occasion, his wife came to me with one of my

own dresses (I was still in my one filthy and ragged dress), and asked me if I would alter it to fit her! Maybe I should have done so, it would have been charitable and a witness to all I believed, but I am afraid it was a very disgruntled missionary who refused to do it. It just seemed like the last straw!

What was it the writer to the Hebrews said? ". . . and took joyfully the spoiling of your goods, knowing in . . . heaven a better and enduring substance" (Chapter 11: 34). And took *joyfully* — as this text came to mind I felt very convicted. It would have been nice to say here that I went to the woman and offered to do it for her, but she had gone elsewhere and the opportunity of turning the other cheek was gone.

This incident really had me thinking how true it is that we hold on to what is ours, in personal belongings and money matters. The Lord had to bring me even further on this matter of taking the spoiling of my goods joyfully. I asked how it could be, but found that He gives grace even for that.

A lot of the things we had in our house were given to us by friends, and there was always the sentimental attachment apart from the value and usefulness of the things. I am sure that is why a missionary home always seems to be a place of peace and happiness, as though the presence of the furniture and furnishings emanate the love of the giver.

We had lost contact with the outside world, I had lost my friends, and now I was to see our house and the little hospital I had founded in ruins. All ties were being severed one by one. I was beginning to learn what it was to be completely dependent on the Lord.

Monday came, and the swelling of my feet and legs had partially subsided. It was agreed that I should go with Lieutenant Dieu-Donné and four other armed Simbas and find my suitcase.

On the way we ran into a group of Simbas who were very obnoxious to me, and it took all Dieu-Donné's time to keep them under control. Of another group we met, several of them had on our house aprons, one had one of my bath towels round his neck, and yet another a blanket of Mary's in a bucket. Dieu-Donné asked if anything belonged to me; if so, I was to take it if I wanted it. I took the towel and the blanket. The Simbas were furious, but I was elated at such a find.

As we neared our village we had to pass several other villages, and the last one immediately before Bopepe had been gutted. Dieu-Donné said it had been done in reprisal for me. We finally arrived at Bopepe. It was deserted, but no wonder! Every house was burnt to the ground except the three with a permanent roof, Bo's, Pastor Asani's and ours, and the church.

We went first to our house, and I was horrified at the wanton destruction. Everything they had been able to take had gone, but the large things like the 'fridge, the stove, dining-room table, the treadle sewing-machine, had all been ruined by machetes. Foods which had been in tins had been poured out on the floor. Books in English, because they could not read them, were just torn up and strewn all over the floor. I found a Bib'e, more or less intact, and a few other books, in particular several medical textbooks, and these were put on one side to go back with us.

We went into the forest and retrieved the suitcase. Also there were several items such as a camp-bed, water filter and primus-stove. The Simbas wanted to take them, but I asked Dieu-Donné to leave them for the villagers as they had lost so much because of me. He agreed, and refused to let the other Simbas take anything but my case. I hoped Bo would be able to make his way through and pick up his things.

There was time to look at the ruined village now, and I felt as though my heart was weeping, I had such a pain in my chest. Previously always a lively village, it was now deserted, and as each house was in ruins, I wondered where the owners were. George, my nurse, had five small children; Mikaele had four little ones, the last having been one of my premature babies; where were they? The houses of the village elders were also gutted – men who had lived saintly lives, hard-working and brave. I wanted to cry, it hurt so much. Dieu-Donné stood behind me and said very quietly, "It was all your fault for hiding in the forest." If he wanted me to have a sense of guilt, he succeeded. I asked, more in anger I suppose than curiosity, "And what profit has this given you, and the cause of the People's Army? Do you really think that such unnecessary destruction of innocent people's homes is going to endear the population to your cause?" He had no answer.

On our return I found that white ants had invaded the case, but only just, and we were able to clear them all away. The Major's wife was with me as I tipped out everything for inspection, and if I had not been quick enough she would have had all those clothes too! As it was she took a cardigan when I was away one day.

That evening I washed and dried like a civilised person and was able to put on clean clothes. Judging by the applause which greeted me it was not before time!

Now I was clean and well clothed, I was told it was time to begin work. It was arranged for me to go to Banalia, twelve miles away, where I would go to the hospital and take whatever was necessary for dispensary work.

After my walk to and from Bopepe, my feet were again very swollen. The Major ordered a bicycle for me, so that I could cycle to Banalia. How did they find a bicycle? Quite simple, they stopped the first cyclist who had a ladies' bicycle and appropriated it! It was a new one, and I felt very sorry for the owner; he had more than likely saved for months to buy it.

We set out for Banalia at six o'clock one morning. The Major told me to pack toilet things and a blanket as we would stay overnight. I was still sleeping in all my clothes, so nightwear was unnecessary. In the toilet line, I lacked two things: a comb and toothpaste, the Major having appropriated both of mine. I reappropriated them and I told him afterwards, and he just laughed.

About thirty Simbas including the Major were going to

Banalia. The Major had on a long button-through dress, beige, with large red buttons, which reached to his feet. He walked all the twelve miles to Banalia in it!

It was wonderful being able to cycle ahead of the crowd, for as I went I could pray knowing I would be undisturbed; it was a pseudo-freedom, but I made the most of it.

At one village where I stopped for a drink of water, Mary Baker's suitcase was on the verandah of a house. She had put all the mission accounts in it and it had been taken to prison with us. All hope I had of finding any of the books were dashed now.

An incident occurred on the way which portrayed the brutality of the Simbas. With the group going to Banalia were two children, a mulatto boy of twelve years and another boy of eleven. These were my unofficial bodyguards. The mulatto boy had been brought up with his white father, but when the troubles began his father went back to his own country, leaving the lad with his mother. He promptly joined the rebel army. A handsome boy, better educated than most of the others, and to a degree civilised, he was polite to me, though occasionally cynical.

He was ahead of me at one part of the journey and pulled up at a village to wait. The few villagers who were there, with the exception of a blind man and his wife, ran into the forest. The boy saw them going, and called to them to come back. They continued without heeding.

The boy, named Panya, that is "the Rat", by the other Simbas, remounted his bicycle and returned to the rest of the group to put in his accusation.

By this time I had reached the village and was talking to the blind man. He was bewildered and frightened when he heard I was white, and he too wanted to hide.

"The Rat" came back with several officers and the other young boy. They were in a fury and grabbed the old man to ask the way to the forest. When I pointed out to them the obvious fact that the man was blind, they left him alone. "The

Rat" then ran into the forest and came back with a young woman who was in an advanced stage of pregnancy. To my utter horror, he kicked her in the tummy, and then hit her on the head with his rifle-butt, screaming at her at the same time to show where her husband was. One of the officers then took over, and hit her several times in the back with his rifle-butt, until she was on the verge of collapse. She took them into the forest, and after about five minutes an elderly man came reeling out, holding his machete. The Simbas then jumped on him, knocking him down and hitting him with their rifle-butts.

The old blind man was terrified, and I led him to the house where he lived. The other Simbas came along then and broke the doors and windows of every house in the village.

I felt physically sick. The man was grey-headed, and his only crime was to be afraid of the Simbas and take to his heels when he saw them coming.

"The Rat" and the other young boy were then detailed to take the man to Banalia *at the run*. He began to run, and "the Rat" would cycle behind him and run his front wheel into the man's legs making him stumble, whereupon the other boy threatened him with a long knife. We were five miles from Banalia, and he was made to run all the way under those conditions, and in the heat of the day.

The woman was also taken prisoner on the same charge, but was allowed to walk.

This is one of the things which we cannot understand about the rebels. They terrorise the people by their brutality, then they are surprised that the people are afraid and want to run and hide.

We reached Banalia, myself beautifully sunburned. A pineapple was shared amongst us, and I was given the largest piece, which was quite welcome after the long hot ride.

How were we going to cross the river? The ferry had been sunk, I knew. I was not left long in doubt. The Major told me I was not to leave him if I wanted maximum security.

He went down to the water's edge, not at the official landing stage, but where we were well shielded by the trees. Air attacks were still a possibility apparently. The Major whistled three times, and was answered by three whistles from the other side. Ten minutes later, two large canoes arrived and we duly crossed.

My heart sank when I saw how many Simbas there were. They had an inspection whilst I was there, and I estimated about two thousand.

I noticed that the "uniform" was no longer the fur pieces, but red strips of material worn either as arm bands, belts, hat-bands or in some cases, round the head, rather as a little girl wears ribbon.

They were openly hostile to me at first, but after the inspection they were very kind, going out of their way to be helpful. I was a nurse and therefore valuable. Too late they realised what they had done in killing our doctor and medical staff.

That day I witnessed a "trial" by the people. Five men were brought out, accused of stealing. The stolen goods, five trunks full of clothes, were also on display.

The first man was called forward and asked to state his case. He said the contents of "his" trunk were personal belongings. The trunk bore the name of one of the Catholic sisters who had been murdered, and her address. It contained habits and church furnishings obviously from the sacristy of the Banalia Catholic church. The man naturally lost his case, and was condemned to prison and to be beaten twice a day.

Each man had the same type of "trial", and each one was obviously guilty, and had the same sentence.

The contents of the trunks were then distributed amongst all those present, the Major taking the largest amount. Before they were allowed to have them, the rebel witch-doctor was called to "baptise" each item. The Major had claimed a pair of long white cotton stockings which had belonged to one of the sisters. He put them on and wore them quite often, regardless of the incongruity of his appearance and the fact that he had nothing with which to keep them up!

At first the Major always referred to me as his white wife, and I was very indignant about it as it gave quite an erroneous impression. Later I realised he had said it to protect me. The other men, thinking I was the Major's wife did not dare molest me. In many ways the Major was kind to me in a crude way; little by little I learned to accept the motive behind it and was then able to disregard superficialities. He always maintained the standard of a Congolese gentleman with me.

Several times when I was threatened by amorous Simba officers, it was a simple matter to take the man to the Major, and always he upheld my cause, and the man would leave hurriedly.

Whilst on this subject, I would mention the confusion in the minds of the pagan Congolese. They understood that a Catholic sister was unmarried, but they could not grasp the fact of a Protestant girl being unmarried, as so many of our women are married, and they thought that the men had several wives, but only those who bore children lived with them!

It made it easier to tell them I was a Protestant sister in much the same way as the Catholic sisters.

The day after our arrival at Banalia I had to rob the hospital. With a strong escort, I went first to the pharmacy. What I saw there dispelled any conscience I had about robbing it. Already there were several people engaged in the same task, but they illegally, as if that made mine legal!

Books, cartons, literature from the boxes were all strewn on the floor. There were hardly any ampoules left, they being the most popular. I managed to take a large amount of very dangerous drugs, including a large stock of morphia. Dressings were few, and there were no bandages. The pickings were comparatively meagre.

Our next stop was the operating theatre – what utter chaos there! Thousands of pounds worth of equipment ruined!

There were comparatively few instruments, but I availed myself of those I thought necessary, and looked around for some linen, towels, etc., but apart from five long operating sheets, all had gone. So too had the beautiful stainless steel sterilising drums so essential to an effective surgery. The Simbas had taken them, finding them useful in place of cases.

Finally we went to the obstetric department, and again chaos reigned. It was heartbreaking to see such wanton destruction because they did not understand the function of each piece of equipment.

On our way back, I called into the wards; all mattresses and pillows had been stolen, and here and there was a poignant reminder of how the patients had fled in haste: a leg splint, a back-rest, a bottle with tubing still attached.

We went back that night to my original resting place with the Simbas. Three trunks and one large box preceded me, carried by forced labour from the village. Not all I had packed arrived at its destination.

One problem I had was finding time to read my Bible. From daylight to bedtime I was in constant demand. They would even ask for my services before I had left my bed in the morning. It did not seem to worry them what time it was, or whether it was convenient, they wanted treatment then and there! Consequently Bible reading was very difficult.

On our arrival back from Banalia, I demanded a room of my own. Apart from the Major's wife, I was the only woman, and although he was amused by my request, the Major turned out several officers from their room and had it cleared for me. Without a twinge of conscience I moved in.

Several of the Simbas wanted to stop me reading my Bible and made a fuss about it, but the Major took my part and told them to leave me alone. He was nominally a Catholic, but had no time for anyone who believed in God. Often he told me that our Congolese pastors were reactionaries and preached against the People's Army.

We opened several bush dispensaries, but as soon as we were in full swing the order would be given to advance, and everything was repacked and moved on.

The work I did was solely medical, and at first they said I could only treat the Simbas, but at this I refused to do any work. The People's Army was fed by the people, and housed by the people, and therefore the people had as much right to my services as the Simbas! Also, as a British trained nurse, I was committed to care for all types of patients, regardless of colour, class or creed, friends or enemies. The latter word made them mad, and I reminded them that I was a missionary and that my Lord also taught me to love my enemies. They then agreed to my treating all and sundry, on condition the Simbas had priority and were seen first in the morning. That was a happy arrangement as the population was scared of them in any case.

Our numbers increased from one hundred to two hundred and fifty a morning, and they gave me a "staff" — one trained nurse from Banalia, a Christian who had been forced to join the army. He had been present when our missionaries had been killed. Several others were so-called Red Cross by virtue of wearing one, but they knew nothing and did not want to know, and were so lazy I despaired of ever coping with the situation. It was obvious to me that they were in it for what they could get out of it, and numerous drugs would disappear overnight.

During this time I was ordered by the Major to wear a red arm band. I refused, saying I did not wish to join the organisation. I was a missionary and therefore owed allegiance to God. They said in effect that it was a lot of bunkum, but left me alone. They said my rank was that of Major — but I refused to answer to it, and that too was eventually dropped in favour of mere "comrade".

One of the things the Simbas believed was that the magic medicine not only made them invulnerable to death, but also to pain, and should they for any reason experience it, all they had to do was to utter the magic formula and the pain would go.

Rather like a form of self-hypnosis, except that it never worked.

Witness two such cases. The first was a tall, strapping fellow in his early twenties, who had a toothache. He was brought in by several sympathetic Simba friends; would I take out the offending tooth? As I peered into his mouth, my heart sank; it was a lower molar, carious, but well and truly embedded. They had destroyed all my local anaesthesia and my dental syringe was gone. I was not really trained as a dentist, but had not minded doing extractions when I had the local anaesthetic to give; but without it I was more scared than the Simba concerned. The situation was explained, but he was so miserable he did not think it could hurt much more!

Facetiously I said that he would have to try his native magic and see how it worked. To my astonishment they *all* agreed.

It took four hefty men to hold him down, and his yells were interspersed with the chanting of the men, "*Mayi, Mayi, Lumumba Mayi*". The tooth came out, to both the patient's and my relief. But he went away sadly disillusioned as to the magical power of his medicine.

The other case was that of an officer with a large abscess which required opening. He was very cocky in assuring me that he did not need a pain-killer, as he had his magic medicine on and would not feel a thing. I went ahead with the preparations, but when the time came to make the actual incision, he suddenly jumped up off the table and ran down the road, leaving his trousers behind! He was caught by several others, and forcibly held down. His imprecations falling on my ears were accompanied with the chanting of the magic formula of those holding him down.

Food was a problem for us all, but in some ways worse for me, for they kept me working at the dispensary and consequently food was never saved for me, and I had nothing with which I could cook even if I had known how. Several days I would be hungry, and one day I remember praying that something must be wrong somewhere, as the Lord had promised to supply all my need, and food was a real need. That particular day, work was finished, it was late afternoon, and I went for a walk to see if I could obtain some food somewhere. I had no money with which to buy some.

Along the road trudged a woman with a baby in her arms; it was the wife of one of our catechists, and the baby was one I had delivered, a very difficult forceps delivery. We hugged each other and exchanged news, though she knew more about me than I did about her. She commented on how thin I was, and asked what I had eaten that day. With a rueful laugh I explained that I was on a search for food. How much money did I have? On hearing that there was not a franc to my name, she untied her money-belt and took out a twenty-franc note and begged me to take it. My embarrassment must have shown in my face, for she added that as sisters in the Lord we were bound to help each other, and I had helped her with her baby, and this way she could repay. She was poor I knew, yet she so willingly gave what little she had. She showed the true meaning of Christian love.

After almost two weeks we were moved to Banalia (not the official side), and I was given the home of one of our evangelists, who was away with Pastor Asani up country, for a dispensary.

It was during this time that Bo Martin came out of the forest and gave himself up. One morning when I came back from washing, the officer-in-charge asked me to go to the front of the house, and there was Bo! He looked so thin and tired, and they were making him sweep the yard in front. Bo was such a personality, that though he had been given the task to humiliate him, he did it as though it was a special pleasure for him. He always did seek to be humble before the Lord, and he probably would have refused to do the job to please the rebels had he not thought it well-pleasing to the Lord too.

He saw me at the door, and I went and shook hands with him. I could have spoken to him but did not want to incriminate him still further. He whispered that he had come out of the forest voluntarily as he was so hungry, and because he knew they were searching for him and did not want to bring reprisals upon others.

His identity confirmed by me, he was marched to the other side of Banalia to await his "trial". Only since the liberation of Banalia in June 1965 has his story come out. His letter to me in September of that year was a master understatement. "They judged me very severely, I thought I would never get out of it alive. But our Lord was always with me, He saved me, and the Simbas let me go in peace without even hitting me." The story, however, is one of a wonderful deliverance by the Lord.

I quote a letter dated September 1965, from the Congo: "After Bo gave himself up, his chief crime, of course, was he had hidden the Mademoiselle in the forest. He had ten judges. They would question him from day to day — the same questions. Why did he hide the white lady? Was she his mother? His sister? He said he remembered that the Lord had said the Holy Spirit would help us to answer when we were brought before judges, so he depended on Him, and gave them the answer 'in the fullness of the Spirit'.

"They would then take him out to execute him, and always at the last moment someone would call them back and he would be put back into prison. They did not beat him. Seven of the judges were against his execution.

"Finally one day they said, 'We are through, we wash our hands of the whole affair. You know we do not approve this man's death.' They all walked out. The three left said jubilantly, 'Now we can all do as we please, tomorrow you will die.'

"That night he did not know how to pray, so he just said, 'Lord, you must choose for me, whether to live or die. I cannot make a choice.'

"Early the next morning there was a knock on his door; a Simba came in and took him by the arm, usually they pushed him around with their guns! He was sure this meant the end.

They led him to the office, instead of the river! He went inside where the major was, and there was a chair. They told him to sit on the chair, again he could not believe his ears. Usually they pushed him down on the floor. Then the major asked twice, 'Are you a Pastor?' He assured them he was. The major then said, 'Last night I was judged. I did not see who judged me, but a large picture of you came before me and a voice said, "Why do you want to kill this man? If you kill him you will die." ' He then awakened, and could not get back to sleep again. *He went on his knees before Bo*, and with folded hands begged him to forgive him for the way they had treated him, and asked him to pray for him that he would not die.

"He went to his typewriter and typed a letter saying that Bo was free, and not to be molested any more! He signed it, handed it to him and told him he could return to his village. When he arrived at his village, the people just gasped, they could not believe their eyes. (Acts 12: verses 14, 15 and 16.)"

I remember Bo being released, though at the time the circumstances of his imprisonment and release were unknown to me. We were watched all the time, and could only exchange general topics, though I did manage to whisper, "Were you beaten?" And he answered in the negative. He asked the next question, "Do you have enough to eat?" I explained the position, and without any hesitation he went off and found a Christian man and his wife who said they would be responsible for my food three times a day.

After Bo left I felt happier, for I had been so apprehensive for him, and it was a wonderful encouragement to my own heart to see how the Lord had undertaken for His servant who had risked his life to save mine.

Shortly after this, I met the "General" and was taken out of the Major's keeping and put under the personal protection of "General Joseph", a young man of twenty-six years. So began another phase of my peculiar prison life.

6

With the General

DURING the time I was at Banalia, I had gone out to a truck to see the driver about taking a patient to Buta, and he told me to wait by a tree until he had confirmed my request. As I approached the tree, there was a blue book wedged in the branches. It looked like one of Amy Carmichael's books and sure enough it was *Edges of His Ways*. My own property too, judging by the inscription inside! I turned to the passage for the day and read words to the effect, "Maybe there is someone who is going through a special kind of trial and you do not think you can take much more, but . . . He stayeth the rough wind on the day of His East wind." It was such a deep source of comfort to me, as I was at that time feeling so very lonely and wondering how long it was to go on.

The next day I was called out to the front of the house, and there were two white men! The Major gleefully pointed to them and said, "Your relatives!" They looked visibly shaken when they saw me too. They had come from Buta where, they said, there were over fifty white people, including many nuns and a Belgian lady and two children. I was flabbergasted, for I had believed myself entirely alone in the area. "He stayeth the rough wind in the day of His East wind".

They were interested in my story, as they had heard all had been killed at Banalia. They were so kind to me, and shared their bread — real bread and, oh luxury, cheese! — with me. They said they nearly always ate European food at Buta, and that on their return they would see the Colonel and ask him to have me sent there.

The two men were from Switzerland and Belgium, and had been brought down to Banalia to repair the ferry. They were of course prisoners too.

A few days later I met the "General", though at that time he was only a Colonel. He had heard about me, and wanted me to go with him nearer to Stanleyville as the need was very great there, with plenty of wounded and sick civilians.

He was a young man, only twenty-six years of age, and had been brought up in an orphanage run by Catholic sisters; at the age of ten he was sent to Belgium where he went through High School and two years in College. He spoke beautiful French as well as Swahili and Lingala. He always addressed me in French.

I was given half an hour to pack my few belongings and the dispensary. He also gave me some money to pay any debts I had incurred, so I was able to pay the Christian couple for all the food they had given me, though the love and companionship was without price.

We left for the other side of Banalia immediately, and once more I was installed in what had been the Administrator's house.

They gave me a room, but it was so situated that it was the highway to the bathroom, and the kitchen too. They also kept the supply of drinking water there. Often I would waken at night and find somebody slaking his thirst. Also, when the General wanted a council of war it was held in my room, regardless of my presence! Another time he "entertained" several brother officers there to supper whilst I was in bed, though not undressed. They spat their fish bones all over the floor which did not help with all the traffic through it.

This house was particularly noisy due to the residence of the General; all the officers came at some time or other, rather like a club. Food was good when we had any!

Under my bed was a trunk with thirty million francs in it— stolen, of course. I felt the need for fresh fruit and asked the

General for some money to buy it, and he gave it to me. In this way I was able to supplement my diet. All this time the African food had been playing havoc with me, and I found I could not tolerate rice; it really made me ill, and if there was no alternative, it meant going without, which was fairly frequent. Remember we ate rice in place of bread and potatoes, and often it was the largest portion of the meal.

We began another dispensary near the river, abandoning the original hospital one as being too far away in case of attack. I met several of the civilian nurses from the hospital, and they really did work well, though I felt sorry for them having to have Simba "nurses" with them.

A man was found dead on a little-used track and I had to go and certify his death. He had been dead a long time judging by the smell and state of decomposition. No questions were asked as to why and how he died; no post-mortem, nobody cared, and he was buried unmourned.

On the contrary, a Simba had a fight with another Simba and was shot dead. He had a military funeral with full honours, and even a gravestone with a gigantic cross above it! I was commanded to attend the funeral, to take flowers and to wail. I refused to do so as the officer detailed to take me was drunk and I did not wish to walk alone with him under such conditions.

I wanted to go to the house where we had been imprisoned in November, and from where our friends had been killed, but entrance was denied me then.

In the other direction, I went to the Catholic sisters' convent. It was all in chaos, their beautiful chapel desecrated. Plain vandalism in every room. The sisters had possessed a lovely cat; I found him dead, all four legs dislocated; he must have died of starvation and in extreme agony.

In one room there was a passport on the floor, and when I opened it the face of one of the murdered sisters looked out at me. Furtively I tore out the photograph, and returned the book to the floor. I would have been beaten if they had seen me with the book. The photograph has since been forwarded to their Mother Convent in Belgium.

From the convent to the Catholic church. Here again, pure vandalism. Nothing remained intact. A beautiful leather-bound book had even had paint poured over it.

I left there and went to the priests' convent and again, everything was destroyed. The Simbas saw me prowling round these places and put them out of bounds to me. They said it was the National Army who had done all the destruction, but the Simba mark was upon it all. l did not argue as it would have been useless, and anyway I had to live amongst them, and wanted to keep a degree of peace between us!

The General decided I was to go to the hospital and muster as much furniture together as possible, such as an operating table, delivery table, trolleys, baby cribs, and so on. There was not much left, but I did as I was told. It was a waste of time. The Simbas later stole everything.

One day there was a truck load of Simbas in from Buta, and they had with them three men who had stolen twenty million francs. Two of them were tortured for four hours and then freed, but the third was tied up in such a way that his elbows and ankles met. He was put on the ground outside my room, and beaten and kicked unmercifully every half an hour for three days and nights. To see him there and be powerless to do anything to help was agony. His screams went through me and made me feel ill.

They laughed at my tender heart as they called it, and said he had stolen all their pay. I realised in a way how mad they were for this was January and they had not been paid since August.

It transpired later that the man was also one of the two officers who had ordered the killings of the missionaries. He died from his ill-treatment. The other had been killed when the ferry was bombed in December.

During the heat of midday I would wander down to the

landing stage of the ferry, and there I found solitude and the heart's ease in prayer. It is a beautiful river, and everything was so indicative of a Sovereign Lord that in spite of heart-ache and loneliness, it became a spiritual oasis for me. Often I could not pray in words, my feelings ran too high, but always I was able to leave this sacred (to me) place strangely comforted and conscious of the Divine Presence.

The day for advance came, or rather the night. At 10 p.m. we packed a Volkswagen Camionette with our things (the vehicle looked exactly like the one we had been going to collect in Stanleyville before the revolution and it was new — maybe it *was* the one, who knows?).

The General, his aide-de-camp, a cheerful major, and the General's "little Simba" called Victor all climbed into the Camionette. The last named turned out to be none other than the little ten-year-old Simba of our prison days. Victor became my bodyguard. We had an outrider, Captain Jean Pierre, but his motor-cycle broke down half way.

We arrived at 2 p.m. at a place called Belgika, about thirty-eight miles from Stanleyville, and two miles past our U.F.M. station of Banjwadi.

From here on, my life became more comfortable. The General found an enormous bedroom for me in a European professor's home. Thankfully I went to bed. I did not undress, from habit I suppose. It was as well, for I wakened in full daylight and found I was the object of inquisitive scrutiny from the four curtainless windows!

They fed me, with food on a china plate, a spoon and a fork, and even a glass of water! The General ate apart from the men always, and was obviously used to a civilised way of eating too — not that I ever heard him complain if he had to eat with his fingers, or drink water from a communal bowl or bucket!

That same morning he came to take me to the Banjwadi station, as he knew it was of my own mission.

It was heartbreaking. The same wanton destruction was here as at Banalia Catholic mission. Gaping holes had even been cut in the ceilings of some of the rooms.

There were several books, but one in particular I noticed lying with all the papers and rubbish, was Geoffrey Bull's book, *God Holds the Key*; I asked permission to take it and it was granted. *There was nothing else of real value to take!*

The buildings were all intact, but absolutely denuded of furniture.

As I came out to the car, a man who had been in the group of bystanders came out from them and grabbed my hand. He was one of our Seminary students who had been stranded during the long vacation. How good it was to see him, and also his wife, and to get news hurriedly from him of loved ones.

They had all fled to the forest after the massacre, but were now slowly coming back to the village. As far as I could gather that day, nobody had lost their life at Banjwadi. They were meeting daily for prayer, and twice a week held a little service in one of the houses.

What that meeting did for my morale is hard to put into words; suffice it to say I returned singing, much to the General's amusement.

The General, whilst he tolerated my religious views, refused to let me talk to others about them, as it was "reactionary".

Later that same day, we went to a beautifully-furnished home in a rubber plantation. This was situated approximately twenty miles from Stanleyville, just before a fork in the road, the right-hand fork being the new main road into the city, and the left-hand one the old and seldom-used route to the same city. It was this latter which the Simbas used, and along which they kept most of their arms and supplies.

The General left me in this home in the charge of a major and his wife. They were kindness itself. The General also loaned me his radio, and the first thing I heard was the announcement that Winston Churchill was very ill. He died the following day.

I was able to take time off from work to follow the B.B.C. commentary on the day of the funeral.

I wondered if there had been a memorial service at home for me, and tried to visualise their faces when they found out I was alive if they ever did!

Here we set up yet another dispensary in the basement, and we were well patronised. It was hard to see little children starving and ill, for there was no food to give them, and precious few medicines. I could only whisper to them of the Great Physician.

My sortie from here was in the trailer of a farm tractor; I felt most undignified clambering up and into it, and off again when we arrived at Bengamisa, thirty-two miles from Stanleyville.

Here quarters were not so luxurious and I was back in the first Major's house. I had a room to myself. Here too, food was scarce, and often I had a meal of only raw peanuts.

In this house, the "bathroom" was outside and in full view of everybody, including the road. I refused to live in the house unless something was done about it. They were furious, but within two hours it was all closed in with sheets of aluminium. Where they found them, I do not know. That was not my worry!

Here the staff allocated to me was large and included several young thirteen- and fourteen-year-olds. There was liberty in speaking to them, and often when the dispensary was closed we would sit round a large table and hammer out our theories to each other. Mostly they listened attentively as I talked to them of Christ and His way of life, and all but one agreed it was good. The one was a fourteen-year-old who would not utter a sentence but that he wanted to kill somebody. He "pooh-poohed" Christianity with all the scorn of a born atheist. He knew his "party-lines" perfectly but would frequently be told to shut up by the others who thought he was an extremist. He was just fourteen years old! It is a sad reflection on us as Christian teachers that not more youngsters are so devoted to Christ.

One day, whilst busy at the dispensary, I heard screams from men, and the heartless laughter of others. On inquiry, nobody would tell me the cause, so I went to investigate.

Before my horror-stricken gaze, there lying in a row in the road were five men. They had each received the special "command" treatment of the Simbas — arms crossed and tightly tied behind them at elbows and wrists; legs crossed and ankles tightly bound, and a cord passed from the ankles to the elbows pulled tight, so that the bodies were pulled into an oval shape, back bent backwards. They were then kicked and beaten about the head and shoulders. The road was dusty, their faces were pushed into it.

What was their crime? They were civilians, one of whom had kept a little shop at Bengamisa, where he had sold soap and cigarettes amongst other things. When the rebellion began, he packed most of his stock into cartons and hid them in the forest together with his wife and family and the villagers.

This little stock enabled him to keep the villagers supplied, but somebody became jealous and reported him and said he had stolen the things. He and four of the village men were arrested and treated thus. All the stock was confiscated.

They were left to lie on the ground for five hours in the hot sun, right over the noon-time period. It made me feel sick when I saw them, and the Simbas again laughed at my so-called tender heart.

At the house one night, a Simba played Viola Walker's accordion, the same four bars over and over again, until I was almost at screaming point. If I had asked him to stop, he would have carried on longer and louder to retaliate. I was lying on my bed trying to sleep — I prayed and asked the Lord to stop him, or else give him another tune. Within three minutes he stopped playing and left. How slow we are to ask the Lord for everyday things!

Another day I longed for some eggs, and knew the possibility of buying any was nil. Again I prayed and asked for some.

That same afternoon, a Simba came with four eggs he had been given for me!

Soap was getting very low. I had a little piece left. I asked the Lord for soap – after all, He had promised to supply my every need – and that same day the major gave me three bars of Sunlight soap, and two bars of toilet soap.

The Lord was answering so many of my *little* prayers, yet it seemed as though He would not answer the one big prayer for deliverance. I had asked Him for Christmas Day, then New Year's Day. Now I asked for my birthday, April 5th – "After all Lord, You've had plenty of time to get the National Army organised if You want to do it that way;" thus I reasoned with Him. Strangely, I could never find real assurance about this as I did praying for other things.

I did not forget to ask Him to burden somebody at home for me, and would name certain individuals who I knew would really pray if they thought I was alive. As for being liberated, I guess there was a lot more for me to learn before I could be freed. It is amazing to what lengths the Lord will allow us to go in order to teach us something. I think my lesson was for patience – "Knowing this, that the trying of your faith worketh patience. But let patience have her perfect work, that ye may be perfect and entire, wanting nothing" (James 1: 3 and 4).

One afternoon, the General came to collect me to go to Banjwadi for a social evening. I wondered what was in store for me!

As we turned into the driveway, it was obvious that the station had been tidied up and the long grass cut. Every house was occupied, not with rebels, but with civil administrative staff, that is, those appointed by the General to run the territory. Newspapers were gummed on to the windows to remedy the lack of curtains. The electricity was running, but they complained that the water system had broken down.

Our "host" for the evening was none other than the District Commissioner, alias "Monsieur, the Devil" of our prison days!

He was charm personified. He had lost his beard – the National Army had shaved him in Stanleyville – and had no glasses. He remembered me, and could not do enough to make me welcome in "his home", which really belonged to the Mission, and had been the house occupied by the Muchmore family before they went home on furlough.

There was apparently to be a Council of War amongst high ranking officers, and they were to meet at 8.30 p.m.

Chairs were brought out on to the spacious lawn at the back of the house, and native wine was served, also cigarettes to the accompaniment of background music of the cha-cha-cha type. It was absolutely nauseating to have to sit there with them, but there was no option, as medical work was on the agenda and I had to take part.

Afterwards we went into the house, and there I met two civilian nurses, who hated the regime and were trying to work their way to Stanleyville. As I was standing talking to them, I heard someone calling me, and lo! everybody was seated at the table but myself – and "Monsieur, the Devil" was patiently waiting for me with a chair! It was all so ludicrous.

He himself waited upon me at the table, and we had roast beef, whole chunks of it, plus rice, manioc, plantains, and delicious gravy. The fellow who had cooked had been a cook to a white man before the rebellion.

By the time we left, it was 11.30 p.m. and I was staying eight miles away. The General saw me "home"; he came right into the house with me (we had guards of course), and as I went into my room with the matches to light my palm-oil makeshift lamp, I heard somebody jump up from my bed and yell, "Don't light the light yet, Mademoiselle, I must put my trousers on first!" The General was having hysterics outside the door. The Simba, having decided I was not going to come back to sleep, had decided to utilise the bed, as it was much more comfortable than the floor which he normally occupied!

Two nights later, the General sent for me to transfer to a

place just two miles from our station of Banjwadi. It was a technical school, and went by the initials E.T.S.A.F.F. and was always referred to as "Etsaff". The time was midnight and I was in bed, partly undressed.

Happily, I did not possess much, and soon packed and arrived at Etsaff at 1 a.m. The General had been called away, but had left orders for me to occupy his own room in his absence.

It was, of course, a white professor's home, and the General had somehow managed to preserve it intact. We had running water and electricity, a stove that worked, and even a gas stove and refrigerator.

Food varied—sometimes plenty, sometimes nothing at all.

The General was used to eating much as we do, that is, at a table with a knife and fork. The home we occupied had all we needed to live a civilised life.

It was one of my duties to make sure the house was properly run. Often we would have rebel officers in to lunch or supper. They were not used to eating at the table, and would spit their bones, either chicken or fish, on to the floor surrounding them. It was therefore a definite chore to pick up these bones at the end of the meal.

I tried to put an empty plate on the table on which to put their bones, but this failed. They saw the empty plate and promptly gave it back to the "boy" with instructions to fill it!

Another time, while we were at the table (I always insisted on eating with them rather than in the kitchen to which I was relegated as a woman), the officer opposite me decided I did not have enough on my plate, so grabbed a handful of meat and spinach and reaching over, placed it in front of me. It was a delicate situation. To refuse food when offered is a virtual insult, but I was not very hungry, and also I was not sure if the fellow had washed his hands. The General was amused; he spoke to me in French which the officer did not understand. He said it was an interesting situation, he was terribly amused and was watching to see how I would extricate myself without insulting the man. The wretched man watched every mouthful I ate, making comments as to the small amounts I placed in my mouth, as to how slowly I ate. Why did I eat with a spoon *and* a fork?

All rather funny in retrospect, but awfully embarrassing at the time.

Once more I founded a dispensary although there had been one here, but everything was stolen. My "staff" were duly transferred.

One case in particular I remember was that of a wounded Simba having spent four days on the road, who came to me with a compound fracture of his lower leg. A compound fracture is a broken bone complicated by a wound which has direct contact with the bone. It was grossly infected. We were without penicillin or any drug which would combat the infection. We had plaster of Paris, which I had stolen from the hospital, and a very few dressings. We gave him a spinal anaesthetic and cleaned up the wound; the bullet had gone clean through the leg and out the other side. We then put his leg in a good position and put on the plaster of Paris.

Four days later his leg was worse, the infection spreading. It was obvious I would have to open the leg further up, as I thought there was a large abscess. When it was opened, there was another bullet! It had lodged about three inches above the entry of the other one. He made a good recovery, and was walking with sticks when I was re-arrested in May.

A large number of officers and Simbas had advanced to our U.F.M. headquarters just outside Stanleyville, and they said I was to join them later. My feelings were mixed at this news, for although it would be nearer the National Army, I knew they would do all in their power to prevent me meeting them. "Don't worry," they would assure me, "we won't let the enemy find you; if we retreat, you retreat with us." The "enemy" were my friends, I knew!

One of my jobs was to reopen the Banjwadi maternity. The two civilian nurses were there, and were coping well, but they could not, as men, do the obstetric work. Twice a week I would walk to Banjwadi.

Apart from the maternity and child welfare work I could do, it was lovely to be able to slip away at the end of the clinic and see my friends. I would tell my guard to wait for me at the station entrance, and could then visit them alone.

There was an elderly man there, who had been a house-boy for many years, and it gave me a real thrill to see him and his wife alive. They were tearful and had suffered much, but they were more concerned about us. The first time we met, I was terribly hungry, not having eaten for twenty-four hours. I hated asking for food, but did so, and was glad I did on two counts: firstly, they had some to give me, and secondly, it gave them so much pleasure to be able to give me something, that I was glad I had asked.

Before I left, they loaded me with sweet potatoes, payapaya — a large soft fruit, rather like a melon to look at but not so sweet and juicy — and bananas.

The other Banjwadi folk came round, and we had a rich time of rejoicing and fellowship together. It was lovely to be able to pray freely with one another.

After that, whenever I went there, one of the families always had something cooked for me.

The day came, late in February, when the General said I was to go with him to Buta, approximately one hundred and seventy miles away. Ostensibly, it was to obtain supplies for the dispensaries.

True to all rebel activities, nothing went according to plan. We were due to start at nine o'clock on Monday morning, and we left at ten on Wednesday night.

We set out heading a small convoy, with one outrider, whose name was Captain Jean-Pierre.

After two miles, our car broke down and we transferred to a

small van; after twenty miles, the outrider's motor-cycle broke down. We reached Banalia at 2.30 a.m. The Administrator was called, and it was the same one from my prison days. He greeted me as a long-lost friend, and hastened to do the honours as a host. It was the same house as before and I knew my way round!

At 3.30 a.m. a scrumptious meal was on the table, elephant meat, rice and pounded plantains. They only had one knife and fork and I was honoured with them! The Administrator had taken all our knives from us when we were in prison, and here he was insisting I have the use of them first! How times change!

We left Banalia at daybreak, 5.45 a.m. After ten miles the back wheel of our van came off and we once more transferred, this time to a large eight-wheeled truck. It was hot and sticky, and it did not help that somebody had presented the General with a baby owl, and I had the privilege of caring for it on the journey. When I am hot, my hands perspire heavily, and the poor bird looked in a sorry state after an hour or two of my handling!

Another thing for which I was responsible on that journey was a bottle of Scotch whisky. The General had asked me to look after it, as I was the only one he could trust not to drink it en route!

We passed Bopepe village, but it looked deserted. I recognised several people in the ensuing villages. About nine miles past Bopepe is a large plantation called Zambeke, and it was here we were scheduled to stop whilst the General inspected the troops.

As I dismounted from the truck with the owl, I left the whisky under the seat. I was recognised by several women who had been standing around. They seemed overjoyed to see me, as I them, and one of them volunteered the information that many of the Bopepe folk were in the vicinity. She went off to find them for me.

I was terribly apprehensive as to how I would be received by the Bopepe-ites, as it is one of the customs in our part of Congo to give "an eye for an eye and a tooth for a tooth". I had been the unwitting cause of the death of two men of the village, several wounded, and all homes lost. How would they receive me? I was afraid, no, not of physical violence, but of mental pain. Would they hate me?

I was seated with the General (and the owl) when somebody came in and asked him if I could go outside as some women had arrived and wanted to see me. I hurried out of the house and there they were! Why did I ever worry about how they would receive me?

Alphonsina put her child on the ground, ran to me, flung her arms round my neck and wept on my shoulder. Cecilia took my hand in the two of hers and she too was weeping. Then others came; the Simbas were mad at them for crying, and they stopped, but it was a wonderful reunion. Not only had I seen my precious friends again, but I feel that I witnessed a miracle, for I asked Alphonsina, "Do you not have any hate in your heart against me for all the sorrow and loss you have suffered?" She answered so simply and sincerely, "Mademoiselle, what we have lost can be replaced, the Lord is able to supply all our needs, but if we had lost you after what happened at Banalia, I don't know what we would have done. Please don't worry, it's we who worry and pray much for you." I was comforted. She then went on to ask many questions pertinent to my life with the Simbas. They had heard many ugly rumours about me, and I was glad to be able to relieve their minds. It was good, too, to have up-to-date news of Bo Martin and all the others.

The Simba who had been delegated to guard me did not like the way the women would grab me every now and then, but I explained that these were all my special friends. The women took it up then. One held up her child and said, "This is one of Mademoiselle's babies," then another said, "Look at me, didn't she make me better in her hospital?" and so on, all making their own personal claim. The Simba went in and the General and the owl came out; he stood watching, amused, and finally made the comment that I had more friends than he did!

The villagers fed us, and afterwards the General inspected the troops. There was not one rifle! They all had a piece of wood fashioned roughly into the shape of a rifle. The commanding officer had on one of Viola Walker's sun-hats, back to front, decorated with Christmas tinsel and fine white wiring, probably from a transistor radio aerial. He was almost drunk.

After the inspection, we made our way back to the truck, surrounded by dancing women, followed by the troops chanting some words about the General and his bravery in battle. He had never been in battle!

The journey continued. The owl refused all nourishment and was back in my hot, sweaty hands. The whisky I conveniently forgot; it was still under the seat.

The tedious journey went on. The General told me he was going to resign from the army and be the political man, and see to the economics. I was surprised, but happily held my peace.

At 4 p.m. we stopped for water and bananas at a village forty miles from Buta. I had perspired so much, and my clothes were so wet, it was possible to wring them out. Whilst we were in the village, a car arrived from Buta, a beautiful Cadillac. The Colonel at Buta had become impatient and had sent on an officer to find us and to hurry us through. I was not averse to riding in a Cadillac, especially after the truck, and our things were then transferred, including the owl and the whisky, the latter being put into my hands again for safe keeping!

The driver of the Cadillac was a Commander, and drove recklessly; he happily pointed out the skid marks he had made on the way! I prayed very fervently. The General then, to my horror, offered some whisky to the driver, who drank almost the tumbler full! If I had prayed fervently before, I redoubled my efforts now. The owl must have sensed my misery, for he hopped from the General's shoulder and squatted on mine for the rest of the journey. Perhaps he knew I had a Sovereign Lord and felt safer with me!

The driver had a strange tale to tell. He had been a mere Captain, and had fallen foul of the Colonel. He was condemned to death. He with several others, was taken to the riverside, and the Colonel personally did the shooting. The others were killed, and the driver received his bullet in the back. He must have fainted with fear and pain, was presumed dead and thrown into the river with the others. The water evidently revived him and he made his way out of the river and lay in hiding for a day. His wound was very painful and he made his way to the hospital during the night. He firmly believes, as do all the Simbas, that he had really died, and that the power of the medicine magic resuscitated him. He showed me his wound to substantiate his story; it was a superficial skin wound, and happily for him the bullet had bypassed all vital organs. The General was *most* impressed. I again thought it the better part of wisdom to remain quiet. He was consequently made the Colonel's private secretary and promoted to Commander.

He is only one of many who have a similar story to tell. The Colonel must have been a pretty poor shot, for this was all at point-blank range with a revolver.

Buta! At last we had arrived; it was 7 p.m. as we drove into the Convent of Le Saint Coeur de Marie (The Holy Heart of Mary).

A Congolese nun was despatched to call the Belgian Sister Superior. The General took my things out of the car, handed me the whisky bottle and asked me to keep it until he called for it!

The driver got out to shake hands and to my horror, I noticed he had his right leg in a plaster of Paris; it was obviously broken. It was as well I had not seen it *before* we drove away from the others.

They both went back into the car, without waiting; the

General said he would call for me the next day at midday to go back to Etsaff, and with a wave, they were gone.

As they left the convent grounds, the car overturned; no one was hurt. My prayer for safety in the car had not been unheard!

I stood waiting for the Sister Superior; a Protestant missionary with a large bottle of whisky in my hand! How incongruous it must have looked.

7

In the Convent

THE Sister Superior was not long in coming. Quite simply I introduced myself as Margaret Hayes of Banalia. As she heard the word Banalia, she drew in her breath quickly. "But we heard you were all dead," she faltered. Hastily, I told her how I was the sole survivor and had been with the Simbas since Christmas Eve. She took my hand in hers and took me to their part of the convent. Another sister, Sister Assisia, an elderly woman of nearly seventy years, as she busied herself getting me water and a towel, murmured all the time, *"toute seule, ma pauvre petite"* (all alone, my poor child).

The Superior was waiting for me. I thought I had better clarify my status at the beginning, and told her I was a Protestant missionary. Her answer endeared her to me immediately, "You are a child of God and are in need; we too are children of God and in that sense we are sisters in the Lord."

How can I describe my feelings as I entered the refectory and saw eighteen pairs of eyes turn to me in sympathy and love? It was supper-time, a place had been made for me at an already overcrowded table, and a delicious plate of soup was put in front of me. I hardly knew how to return thanks, words were so inadequate to express all I wanted to say.

Conversation was naturally full of questions. My French improved by leaps and bounds! Nobody knew English; most of the sisters were Flemish, and a Belgian lady – Madame Le Gros and her two little girls, Ann, four years old, and Chantal, six, were French-speaking.

It amazed me to hear the noise at the table, and I made the

remark that I thought they always ate in silence. They laughed heartily at this, and then added seriously that due to the tension under which they lived, the rule was waived. I was grateful for that!

After supper, a shower and clean clothes. I was shown to a room with a hand basin and two mirrors — I had not looked in a mirror for two months! There was a real bed, and a mosquito net too! They asked me if I was too tired to come out and tell the sisters my story. Too tired! I would have sat up all night just to enjoy their company. A bell rang across the quadrangle, but nobody moved, and it was later I found out it was the nine o'clock retiring bell. We talked until 10 p.m.

The Superior took me to my room, and said she would call me at 7.10 a.m. for breakfast. I sat in the armchair and surveyed my surroundings. As I prayed that night my heart was almost too full for words.

For the first time in four months I was able to undress before going to bed. What luxury! It was not long before I fell asleep, and it seemed in next to no time the rising bell of 5.15 a.m. was clanging. I jumped out of bed before I realised where I was, then got back again to wait for dawn in half an hour.

At 7.10 the Superior was at the door; as she knocked, I automatically called out in Bangala asking who was there, and she answered in the same language to her amusement, "*Mama na yo*" (your mother).

Amongst the sisters were three who were nurses, and it was arranged I should go to the hospital with them to try and find supplies to take back with me. The hospital was a large Government one, and in spite of the rebellion, had managed to retain its supplies and equipment.

In the large pharmacy was a big trunk with Dr. Sharpe's name and address on it, presumably stolen from Banalia after the massacre.

My orders completed, howbeit very modified, the sisters

called for me and we were back at the convent in time for diner at 12.30 p.m.

After dinner was siesta-time which was rigidly kept all the time I was with them. Again I slept heavily, awakening only at 3.30, feeling very refreshed. As I came into the main corridor the sisters were coming out of the chapel.

It was a beautiful place, uncluttered, modern, yet in its very simplicity there was a beauty which had to be felt more than seen. The altar was simple. The only decorations were flowers, tastefully arranged, appealing to the aesthetic taste of all present.

The Superior genuflected and crossed herself with holy water; if she expected me to do the same, she gave no outward indication. She gave me an open invitation to all services and times of prayer, and said also I could use the chapel for private prayer any time I wanted. It was an honour, I felt, and accepted it as such.

They had Mass in the mornings at 5.30 and then devotions until 7.10. Next came prayers at midday for fifteen minutes, then 3 — 3.30 p.m. for prayers, 6.30 — 7 p.m., and lastly 9 p.m. for fifteen minutes also for prayer. But often the sisters would be in the chapel at other times too. I went to all except the early morning sessions and the late night ones. As they prayed in Flemish or Latin, it did not disturb me and I could pray in my own way undisturbed.

The children were fidgety and therefore the Superior arranged for an extra place to be put for me apart from them, so that I could pray without the distraction of the children.

During my first five days with them, I heard that two of the sisters had been given permits to go over the border and on to Europe for a two-month vacation, but that thus far nothing had materialised. The Colonel was under the impression that they were all contented to be there, and as he knew it was a European practice to have a vacation, he offered to arrange transport for two sisters and two fathers to go home, and when they came back, he would double the number for the next trip!

On the fifth day the Superior came to my room during siesta and said a jeep had come for me to take me back to Bengamisa. Hastily I gathered my things together and went out to the jeep. The officer was unknown to me, and he said he had been told by the Colonel to take me right through to the most advanced post. Hastily I gave my name and address to the Superior in case the sisters were allowed out of the country.

It was a nightmare journey; breakdowns, men being beaten for nothing at all, the night spent in a village where every man became drunk.

We arrived at Banalia in the middle of a riot. Everything was confusion. Apparently the day after we had left Etsaff the National Army had begun to bomb the area, and the house where we had stayed had received a direct hit. The timings of the Lord are always so right. The General's A.D.C. had put what he found of mine into a suitcase, and had brought it with him to Banalia.

Air-raids were on all the time they said, from 6 a.m. to 6 p.m. The officer with me did not know what to do with me, but finally decided to go on. He was a little man and over his grey-green uniform was a brightly-coloured moslem gown; it looked quite ludicrous with his uniform cap and rifle.

We rode on and on into the night, and finally at midnight arrived at Bengamisa. The night watch were called to find me accommodation and as I looked at them, they were my "medical team".

There was nowhere to put me on my own, so they said I could go to the "ladies-house" – a mud hut, in which were sleeping eight women; one was asked to vacate her mattress, and with due solemnity it was offered me. I was tired, hungry and filthy from the dust on the road, but who cared?

As I lay down I had plenty of time to wonder why the Lord had allowed me to spend five days with the sisters, with all the comparative luxuries of a civilised life, and then brought me out from it into even worse conditions than before. It did not make sense to me, and I grinned ruefully to myself in the dark as I recalled what Paul says in the Epistles, "I have learned in whatsoever state I am, therewith to be content" (Philippians 4: 11). I asked the Lord to make me content.

Next morning they found me an empty house, empty because it was not quite finished. The room allocated to me as a bedroom did not have a window, and so I had to sit outside under the surveillance of my guards to read my Bible, and whilst I did so they would whisper together and prevent anyone from entering!

Two of the guards went all-out to seek my comfort, and the way they cooked was superb. They had both been house-boys in Stanleyville before the rebellion. I thanked God for this extra provision, though it was hard not to think of the folk in Buta and wish I was there too!

The third evening in this environment we were sitting together discussing the Christian life, when a runner came through to say the Major was on his way and I was to be ready to go with him to Banalia. He came along at 10 p.m. He had waited till dark to travel because of the air-raids. We had not had any at Bengamisa, but they recommenced the day after I left. Later I heard that they thought I had some magic power, but I gave all the praise to the Lord.

We travelled through the night on a large ex-mail truck; it was fairly new, and the cabin was comfortable. The Major had brought his first wife in the cabin too. We reached Banalia at daybreak.

It was considered too dangerous to cross on the newly-repaired ferry as our truck was bright red, and air-raids had been on all the previous day.

There was a terrible fight between our Simbas from Buta and the Banalia ones, over the distribution of rifles. I was ushered into the house where we had all been imprisoned in November, and there was a man lying on the floor in the process of being tied up in the special Simba "command" manner. His screams were awful. I asked permission to leave the house but did not know where to go as they were fighting. They took me to the house that Dr. Sharpe and family had occupied, now denuded of furnishing. Who should be there but "Mr. Jingle" of our prison days, but now not so cocksure nor so incoherent. He assured me of his personal attention should any of the Simbas bother me!

Arrangements were then made for me to cross the river in a canoe and to wait there for the Major. We duly crossed, and I was led to a house near the ferry. There were several ladies there, including the Major's three wives, and the lady of the house.

The Major arrived soon after. Not long after his arrival, some Simbas came and told him that the Banalia Simbas had taken our truck and hidden it. The Major was furious and went back over to the other side. We heard shooting. They then brought me a young fellow who had been shot through the hand, shattering most of his bones. I rendered first-aid, and then dispatched him to Buta.

I made my way down a private path to the river and took off my shoes and stood in the water. It was so lovely and cool and my feet were hot and dusty. It was very quiet and peaceful, as I sat on the grassy bank with the water lapping at my ankles. The sun was setting, the sky was cloudless, the shadows were long and the opposite bank was bathed in golden sunlight. I looked at the landing stage over there, and thought about my friends who had laid down their lives. It all seemed so unreal.

In his book, *God Holds the Key*, Geoffrey Bull pens these lines which he composed whilst in prison in China:

> O Lord to know, amidst this tangled skein
> Of men events and things, 'tis not in vain
> I seek that cord of gold, Thy way decreed —
> Is comfort to my soul, O God indeed.

To know amidst this maze of circumstance,
Dead ends which cruelly stay desired advance
Can turn my feet to tread with surer sense
Thy way of truth — Brings peace when all is tense.

To know that when these floods of grief subside,
Throughout the soul's poor fields, the ebbing tide
Must leave such silt as shall much fruit ensure —
My soul sustains and says to faith, "Endure".

So Lord I shall not fall, I shall not faint,
Thy grace enough for every baffled saint,
Still through the wind-thrashed seas, I glimpse Thy form
And know Thou hast Thy footsteps in the storm.

I had learned them by heart and put them to music, and now
by the water's edge, when all seemed so futile, I sang them
quietly. The author of those words had so adequately expressed
how he felt in prison in China, and strangely enough they were
comforting the heart of a prisoner in Africa! As I sang the last
line, I caught a glimpse of the Eternal Majesty of God, and
then almost automatically began to sing that lovely hymn of
praise "How Great Thou Art". Afterwards I made the most of
my solitude and prayed again asking to be delivered in time for
my birthday, and at the same time that the Lord would enable
me to get back to Buta. I had assurance for the latter request,
but not the former. There was still much for me to learn.

The Major came back, this time with the truck, and he said
I could stay at Banalia in the house we were then in. The house
did not have one inside door, and as I knew that several men
would be sleeping there, I told the Major I would not sleep
there but would go back to Buta. Without any further argument he said, "Go ahead, jump in the truck, we are on our
way." I praised the Lord and jumped in as requested.

We stopped for the night at the place I had met the Bopepe

women before, but they were all in bed as it was almost midnight. The Commander's wife gave me her spare bedroom and thankfully I went in and locked the door. About an hour later, I heard the Major asking for me and was glad I had locked the door. He tried it several times, and eventually they told him to leave me alone as obviously I was asleep. I thanked the Lord for that deliverance too!

The following morning we were to move on early, but it was midday before we did so. We stopped at a place called Kole, which is near our mission station of Bongondza. Somebody recognised me and came and told me that Bo Martin had been through there just the day before with his wife and family. He assured me he was in good health.

The wife of the Major was drunk when we entered the truck again, and the Major was sleepy. At one stage his wife had her head on my left shoulder asleep, and the Major had his head on my right shoulder asleep! Once he leaned against the door in his sleep and it flew open and I just managed to grab him in time.

We came to a muddy patch on the road. Other trucks had been ahead and it was churned up and slippery. The Major pulled out of his pocket a special stick of Simba magic medicine, and holding it up in his left hand at shoulder height, he made queer passes at it with his right hand, at the same time chanting: "*Mayi, mayi, Lumumba mayi, advancez, mayi, Lumumba.*" Its magic did not work (maybe because I was on board?) and we bogged down in the mud. His wife made fun of his magic formula, and suggested he had his magic recharged like they do the batteries. He answered her not a word!

As I left the truck I went down to almost my calves in mud. Thick, orange, sticky mud! Ugh! I made my way to the nearest house, and the lone occupant gave me water to wash my feet, legs, and sandals. I was hungry; we had not eaten all day, and it was now 4 p.m. The Major bought some dried fish, and we ate it raw. He also bought a large bottle of native wine, and put it on my lap; I passed it to his wife in exchange for three radios she was carrying.

We arrived at the convent at 9 p.m. Was I glad to see them again! The Superior said they had prayed so much for me to be sent back to them and now the Lord had answered the prayer.

They had kept my room prepared for me in faith, and after a meal of rolls and cheese, and a large pot of tea, I thankfully retired for the night.

The convent was to be my home for three months. As the newest arrival, and "non-professional", they used to call me the Protestant postulant! Madame Le Gros was also teasingly called a postulant, much to her children's disgust. We shared dining-room duties between us, washing up and laying the tables and keeping the place clean.

Madame had experienced a sad time before coming to the sisters. The Simbas had told her in November that they had killed her husband and thrown him in the river. The children were told only that he was in prison. Poor Madame, she was very nervous, not unnaturally, and if a Simba showed his face in the convent, it was enough to send both her and the children scurrying inside the house to hide. The children were dreadfully spoilt by all and sundry, and it was almost more than Madame could do to control them. Yet under the trying circumstances, they were not too bad.

The sisters, at the time of my arrival, were of two different orders, The Holy Heart of Mary, and the Order of the Holy Sepulchre. Most of them were teachers, the majority being university graduates. The others were nurses with the exception of the eldest sister, who had been in Congo for over forty years, Sister Fredeganda, who was the cook.

Whilst I had been away, the two sisters who had been promised a vacation had gone and they very kindly wrote to Mission Headquarters telling them I was alive and well. When this news was given to me, I was so relieved, and knew that folks at home would begin again to pray for us.

My second arrival at the convent was on a Sunday. The following Tuesday a truck came in bringing six Congolese sisters; they had been in the forest for three and a half months, without a change of clothes. Their white habits were dark brown! They had a wonderful story to tell of the Lord's protection.

The following week another truck arrived, and in came three white sisters accompanied by a white brother. The last three months had been an awful ordeal for them, and they were very glad to be with so many other white people. These were sisters from the Ursuline Order. In all we made twenty white people in the sisters' convent, and there were thirty-five white men in the men's convent, as the two men previously mentioned in Chapter 6 lived in the town.

Our convent made bread for them all every day. Our own community also had twenty-four Congolese sisters, and the men's had eighteen Congolese fathers and brothers.

Several of the priests spoke English and would come over to talk to me, bringing me English books to read.

The pervading atmosphere of the convent was one of peace, deepened by a sense of oneness we had in the fellowship of suffering, and for me, though I could not worship as they did, nor could I accept their doctrines, underneath all this there was a bond of fellowship with them, for we all loved and served the same Lord.

Not once did they try to impose their doctrines upon me. We had many discussions. I realised I knew more about the Catholic faith than they did about mine, and they were always very interested to hear. One evening, the Superior asked me how I became a missionary and I explained first how I had become a believer, then how the Lord led me on to fuller service. She was most interested and asked me if I would tell the other sisters that evening at recreation, which I was only too glad to do.

The sisters were a grand crowd, they had a good sense of

humour and loved fun. One day I commented on this and said in effect that we all had the impression that they were always very grave and seldom laughed. They laughed and said it was the opinion they had of the Protestants! They added that they had so much about which to be happy that they had to rejoice all day long. "True," they said, "most people outside the convent only see us in church or in the street and we have to be serious then."

They were disciplined. Not once in all the four months I was with them—and the last month we were under great stress—not once did I ever hear a cross word between them. If they had a difference of opinion they would agree to differ, or one would finally give in, but with very good grace.

My main work during this time was the making of epaulettes for the senior Simba officers. One sister who had gone to Europe had made them, and as I had taken her place at the table, plus her named serviette pochette, they said I could take over her work too.

I was only too thankful to have something with which to occupy my hands. Every day after we had washed up the breakfast things I would go to the machine and make epaulettes. At first they varied in colour and shape but later we standardised them. It seemed that every Simba we met was an officer! As I had gone to Congo as a missionary first and foremost, I asked the Superior if she had any tracts or pictures of Christ. A sister was dispatched to find some, and she showed me several pictures of Christ, and some of Mary, but another sister saw them and said, "Oh, Mademoiselle won't be wanting the ones of Mary!" I chose a picture of Christ surrounded by people of all nations. These would go out in each packet of epaulettes I made. We all prayed that the Simbas' thoughts would be directed to Christ Who alone could give them the real liberation they sought.

Often the Simbas from Bengamisa would come in to see me; two regular visitors were Captain Jean-Pierre, the motorcyclist outrider of the General, and young Victor, the little Simba who had been our guard in prison in November, and was later in the General's retinue. One day a group of Simbas came, nine of them, all officers, and with them was Lieutenant Dieu-Donné of Christmas Day, the one who had played carols to me.

When the Simbas came I was allowed perfect freedom in speaking to them, and often they would ask for a portion of the Word of God, but I did not have any to give them. The sisters gave me a few books on the life of Christ in Lingala which I was able to give away.

The convent owned several animals, including cows, goats, pigs, a monkey, nine dogs, three of them full grown Alsatians, and several cats, the latter rejoicing my heart. The animals had been left by white people and the sisters had just opened their doors to all strays. After a few days the cats were always referred to as "Mademoiselle's cats". I enjoyed teaching the two children how to care for them and they were two willing pupils. We also had a parrot called Koko, and he could speak in five languages, but not English!

One day I had a visit from the man who had driven the car the first time I came to the convent, the "resurrected Commander" – he came to tell me that the General was in prison; he would not say what was the charge, but I am sure it was a trumped-up one. He asked me if I had been the General's wife as that was one of the accusations against him. I was glad to be able to tell him that the General had behaved like an officer and a gentleman as far as I was concerned. The Commander appeared disappointed at my answer, and left me abruptly.

The General was ultimately sentenced to death, escaped from prison, was retaken, and finally shot when the National Army was nearing Buta. I was sorry; he had been kind to me, and had saved several men from death I knew.

The self-styled Prime Minister and President, Gbenye Christophe, paid a visit to Buta; he came from that area. Word was given to the Congolese Bishop that they would have a Mass said in his honour. The sisters all put on their Sunday habits and went across to the Cathedral opposite the convent at the appointed hour of 9 a.m. Madame Le Gros, the children, one sister and I remained behind, watching from the windows. Ten a.m. came and went, and no Gbenye; 10.30 — we heard commands being called and there he was descending from his car (actually it was the Bishop's car). The Simba brass band which was waiting for him in the Cathedral struck up the Congolese National Anthem; it must have been deafening in there! Mass was said, Gbenye was placated, he came out and the band played the only other two pieces they knew well — the Belgian National Anthem, which a priest had been teaching them, and "It's a long way to Tipperary"!

One other time Gbenye ordered Mass, this time a Requiem Mass for those of both sides who had died in the cause of the "liberation of the people".

He also came to the convent and gave a long talk on how well we were being looked after, and how lucky we were to be under the control of the People's Army. If we were called upon to die, well, there would be a martyr's crown for us. Not enough to eat? Why could we not be like our predecessors who ate the grass of the fields?

After this talk, one of the sisters picked a large basket of grass and put it on the dining-room table at supper, and said that all who wished to eat like our predecessors could do so, but she would stick to normal convent fare!

Always there was an underlying current of tension. Reports would come in via the grapevine of National Army activity, and we realised that we were surrounded by them; obviously since the sisters had been able to get out to Europe and tell them of our whereabouts, military operations had intensified.

Another sister was able to get out on April 1st, and she took letters from us all. In May some sisters and two priests were sent over the border for supplies, and they too, took letters. When they crossed the narrow frontier, they were told they could not return, the frontier was closed into Congo. They pleaded to return as their non-return would cause reprisals to be taken. All but one returned, and the one was a priest who had gone further inland to plead our cause to the officials of that land. By so doing, he saved his own life.

Birthdays and feast-days were always made a time of rejoicing, with flowers and some extra luxury for tea. My birthday came and was duly celebrated. There was a lovely bouquet of flowers by my place at the table, and a birthday card I will always treasure. It was hand-painted and showed an open hand from which grew a single flower, a marguerite, and the words on the card said in Flemish, *"In Uw hand Heer, ben ik veilig"* — In Your hand Lord, I am secure. Such a lovely thought when all was in such turmoil around us!

My parents' golden wedding was also celebrated; the priests all prayed for them that morning in the chapel and cathedral. The sisters really went to town and celebrated in a big way. Golden flowers, golden decorations on the table, we all wore a golden leaf. There were songs in English, written by the English-speaking priests. Two sisters dressed up as Mum and Dad fifty years ago, when Dad proposed, and then they had another scene, where they were celebrating their anniversary. It was a hoot and almost brought the house down. Little Ann kept asking, "But where *are* Edward and Louisa?"

My day was divided between work and spending time in prayer and Bible study in the chapel. There was so much for which to pray. The Lord had not answered my prayer for freedom by my birthday, nor by Easter, nor by my parents' anniversary, yet He was constantly answering other prayers. I now asked for deliverance by Whitsun.

The Superior had given me material for a dress, a priest had given me two new dresses from his "poor-box"; we had all the other necessities of life, but we were not free. It was not that we were not praying, we surely were; what was it the Lord wanted to teach us — me?

On Sundays, apart from essential work like washing-up, we did not work. So I would go to my room when all the sisters went to the Cathedral for High Mass. I had made out a little form of service, and would endeavour to have morning worship. My preacher was Geoffrey Bull through his book *God Holds the Key*, and after a few hymns, a Bible reading and prayer, I would read a chapter from this book.

One Sunday I was deeply challenged by the words of this young prisoner-of-war.

I will quote him:

"My avowal surely was 'Lord, I will lay down my life for Thy sake'". Yet the words of the Master still come back: 'Wilt thou lay down thy life for My sake? Wilt thou . . . wilt thou . . . wilt thou?' The days slip by and I become a prisoner of the Communist army. . . . I am taken out by a young official and he talks to me seriously about the question of execution. . . . I am young and it is hard to think of dying alone out there in the hills; and I go back to the dark cell and fight on, kneeling in the dust and the darkness, trying to still my heart-beats and keep back the tears. 'Wilt thou lay down thy life for My sake? Wilt thou . . . wilt thou?'

". . . So then I was going to die and all I know is, that I was not saying any more 'Lord, I will lay down my life for Thy sake'. Not that I would not if I had to, He knows — but only if I had to. It was not my will really to die for Him. The will to live was much stronger. Why was it? Simply that I was facing reality now, and not the make-believe of my daydreams. I had not yet understood the doctrine of departure. We talk about living for Christ. It is more profitable to speak of dying with Him. There are probably too many of us today still living, who should have died long ago."

As I read these words I was startled into thought, and wondered how I had really faced up to this challenge. That day, Christmas Eve, had I really wanted to die? No, I do not think so, I would have done if it had been necessary, but I was glad in many ways that I had not had to go through the valley of the shadow of death whilst still young. The thought appalled me and filled me with shame.

I then read on in the same chapter:
"This then is our heart's trouble, that in the conflict of the cross, we should fail to die. That we should still be in good health, and able to answer questions, when we should have nails in our hands and feet. That we should have survived to face our shame, rather than died in the promise of His glory. That we should be accepted, when we should be outcasts. That we should be accounted friends, when we should be spurned as foes. 'Wilt thou lay down thy life for My sake?'"

That day in my room marked a spiritual crisis in my life. The Lord was teaching me to evaluate life in the light of the cross. Before, my consecration had not been complete; I had thought it had, but now I saw the superficialities of it. I asked to be crucified with my Lord. It would mean humiliation, degradation, self-denying, and dying to self. The Lord was to show me how this was to be. He knows I prayed in all sincerity.

During May, tension began to rise. The Congolese Bishop warned us about making too much noise in the convent, and if we must laugh, to do so quietly, he did not want undue attention being drawn to us.

One day during our last week at the convent, we had a visit from two Egyptians, who were obviously in the propaganda line. They laughed and asked if it was true what the papers had said about all the missionaries having been killed? Of course, there was no answer; we were living proof that not all had died. They took photographs, but we heard later, whether it was true or not, that the cameras were empty. They said they were on a visit to see how Egypt could best help the People's Army in Congo.

The Bishop sent word with one of the priests that if we heard that the mercenaries or the National Army were fifty miles away we were not to sleep in our beds, not to undress, and to be altogether in a small but safe place. He would not disclose what he had heard. Tension was at breaking point. The Congolese sisters were afraid for us, and for themselves too.

The Superior and some others cleared a space in the attic, and put food and other things there in case we had a long siege. Every sister, Madame and I had a case packed and these were finally locked and put together in the store-room, with blankets, pillows, and more food in case of flight or a long overland journey. We did not know what to expect.

All day there would be trucks going past us filled with Simbas, trigger-happy, and thrilled to be going to war. Reports came in that mercenaries had been seen fairly near. Our hopes, though raised for rescue, were constantly watered with the fear of wondering what would happen in Buta.

Everybody spoke in whispers. Madame Le Gros and the children did not go out of the building. My bedroom was changed from being in the front of the house in grand isolation to a cubicle in the large dormitory occupied by the nuns themselves.

Several Simbas came to wish us goodbye, and to solicit our prayers as they went to war. Father Alphonse, a Belgian and the nuns' father-confessor, came over to hear confessions in the chapel. Usually he stayed and chatted until supper-time, but this day he hurried back.

The bell rang at 6.30 p.m. The sisters filed into the chapel, but there were some Simbas in the quadrangle, and Madame would not go out. I stayed back with her, two sick sisters, and the children.

The windows of the work-room, where we had been nearly all day, had been closed but had several peep-holes. I watched the road. Suddenly there was a rush of Simbas down the road behind the cathedral, followed by a jeep filled with Simbas all shouting and gesticulating. *It was the road which led to the men's convent!*

Madame was so nervous, I did not wish to add to it, so kept my observations to myself. Five minutes later we heard shouting and screaming in the quadrangle. One sister turned the key in the lock of our door. We heard Simbas banging on doors and windows, calling us to come out. They went into the chapel and forced the sisters out.

The Sister Superior came to our locked door; we heard her command the Simbas to be quiet, then she called to us to unlock the door. We did so. The room swarmed with Simbas, we were pushed outside aided by spears and rifle-butts. Madame was deathly white; I suppose we all were. The children were so good, and did not even whimper.

"March! March to the men's convent, all of you," they screamed at us. Thus were we arrested on Saturday, May 29th, at 6.45 p.m.

8

Imprisoned again

As we complied with our guards' orders to hurry, I saw the little Simba, Victor, at the corner, waving his spear like a maniac. As I drew near we looked at each other; I was sad to think he was mixed up in this, and was able to say to him, "What, you too, Victor?" He put down his spear and hung his head. We never met again.

The road down hill to the men's convent was full of Simbas, and at the end we saw the pitiful sight of the thirty-one men sitting in the mud on the ground, with their legs crossed. We saw first one, then another, receive the butt-end of a rifle on the head or back of the neck.

We were made to sit behind them in rows of four. Our pockets were searched, and the contents appropriated. I only had a handkerchief, and this was returned. The sisters all had rosaries, as did the priests; these were taken, and broken in pieces before them. Next they demanded all watches, and those who possessed them handed them over to the grasping hands held out for them.

The order to march was given. It was almost dark. We had to walk in twos, and anyone who was too slow was helped along with a push from a spear. The eldest sister, Sister Fredeganda, aged seventy, collapsed twice, and was brutally kicked on the back before she was able to get up.

We walked in silence, though without doubt all were praying hard; I know I was. What does one pray under such circumstances? I prayed, "Lord, we don't understand what is happening, but we believe we are in Your hands, and that You alone hold the key of our lives. We ask only Your grace to go through with whatever is before us now."

The former police station building loomed before us. We lined up in twos in front of it, the priests first. We were then the subject of ribald remarks from the Simbas standing by. Several asked Madame Le Gros, "Where is your husband?" But there was always somebody to answer for her. They asked me where mine was, and when I explained that I was not married, they then asked from where did I come? When they heard the word Banalia, they left me alone.

The next order was for all spectacles to be taken off. I was slow in obeying, so had them knocked off. The sisters then had to remove their bonnets. Several were hit because they hesitated; we could hear the men being searched, accompanied by blows. Slowly the queue moved up.

Eventually it was our turn. One by one we had to step up between two Simbas, and our clothes were searched. Our spectacles were taken, as were the professional wedding-rings and the pectoral crucifixes of the nuns. My heart went out to these women, thus deprived of the symbols which they held so dear. After thirty or forty years a professed nun, it was not always easy to take off their wedding-rings, and we agonised with one sister who almost had the skin taken off with hers.

Finally the search was over, and we were herded together in one room. It was filthy. There were two tables and two benches in it. The priests turned them over to us for our use. We sat or stood wherever we could.

The children were so good, not a whimper, just a tightened hold of the hand indicated how they were feeling.

I could not see very clearly without my spectacles, but I knew there were men standing crowded outside the two windows. Their singing became more meaningful. After about an hour, a major came in with several Simbas and ordered all the priests to undress. They stood in their underpants. Next we were ordered to undress similarly. Several sisters were brutally hit before they complied with the order.

All the clothes were taken and thrown in a corner, and generally mixed up; they really enjoyed doing that.

The priests were then ordered to strip naked. We looked away, but three sisters were forced to watch. The men then were searched for radios and transmitters. Then it was our turn for the same procedure. The Father Superior thought we were all going to be killed then and there, and in a loud voice, and facing the entire room, gave absolution in Latin. Later this was explained to me. The sisters and Madame Le Gros were obviously comforted by this gesture.

The inspection over, they then told us to dress and went out. The men turned their face to the wall and told us to go ahead. As we scrabbled for our clothes and came across the men's we would throw them over to them. It must have looked like a nightmare jumble-sale. If the Simbas had wanted to humiliate us, they had succeeded, but we were not alone in this. Our Lord, too, was humiliated, and He gave us grace to go through with it.

When we were dressed, we women were then led to another room away from the men. There was no furniture, and we sat on the floor. The Sister Superior had fallen two days before and severely hurt the base of her spine; it was torture for her to sit down on the floor, but she did not once complain. As we looked at her with either anxiety or sympathy, she would smile back. The elderly Sister Fredeganda looked ill, but did not complain either.

We had been in this room for maybe half an hour when the door burst open, and in came another major and his retinue of Simbas. Also with him were the Congolese Catholic Bishop, and two Congolese nuns.

This time it was my turn alone to undress, and again be searched for a transmitter, and when I had dressed they called Madame Le Gros to do the same. The Bishop was made to watch. One sister had turned her head away and was struck.

Later we were marched back to be with the men, and the Major then made an accusation against the Bishop, saying that he had been accused of having a transmitter. The Bishop denied the charge, which was obviously trumped-up for the occasion. He asked the fathers to say if he had spoken the truth, and added bravely, "My dear brothers-in-Christ, if you have anything to say in accusation against me, please don't be afraid to say it. I am not afraid to die, and I will forgive you in advance." The Bishop then removed his sash and soutane, and turning to the officer said, "I am ready to die. If I am guilty, shoot me here." The Major laughed and told him to get dressed again, that he had done nothing wrong, and could go back to the convent. Whereupon the Bishop made an impassioned plea that they should take his life in return for those of the fathers. They would not listen, and hastened him and the two Congolese sisters out.

The door was shut, and we were told via the key-hole to get some sleep. Sleep! Nothing was further from our minds! We arranged ourselves as comfortably as we could. Some of the men lay on the floor, using their soutanes as pillows. Some even slept!

There was a fairly wide windowsill, and with four others I occupied it. The Sister Superior was next to me. She looked so pale. There was a small pane of glass missing behind my back, and during the night there was a Simba who came round and shouted at us from outside; he poked me with his spear, and when I looked round, bent down and whispered, "Don't be afraid, you women will all be all right," then hastily straightened up and began shouting again.

Once I was able to ask for some water, but he said he could not do anything until morning. The room was stifling hot. Ann, the four-year-old, began to fidget, she was so tired. Chantal had fallen asleep in a sister's arms. We changed position often, our legs and backs ached. Nobody complained, nobody spoke.

It was quite a strain being without glasses, and it did not help when Simbas would come and point at somebody, demanding their presence outside, as I could not see if they were pointing at me or not. Several of us were in the same plight.

Daylight at last! The guard of the night was changed, and several kind ones were outside the broken window. We managed to get several bottles of water, which were quickly passed round. One officer came in and gave cigarettes to any who would like one. Most of the men did.

Toilet facilities were non-existent, and we were taken outside, two men and two women at a time; we were in full view of each other, the Simbas, and all and sundry on the main road. It seemed they could not humiliate us enough.

Again we were separated from the men, and returned to the room of the previous night. The threats to the men were beginning; as we filed out, they were removing shoes and socks.

We arranged ourselves around the walls. They were covered with yellow distemper, and it rubbed off on to the sisters' white robes and veils.

We were terribly thirsty and asked for water, which was granted, plus two cups. A Simba came in with two mugs of hot milk for the children. They were always kind to them.

Abruptly, the main door to our section burst open and they dragged into a room opposite ours a Congolese. He had been severely beaten, and was unconscious, and one eye had been gouged out. What was his crime? He had sympathised with the fathers.

Naturally we were very apprehensive and could only occupy our thoughts with prayer. We prayed for the fathers, for their captors, for our Congolese friends, and for ourselves. My thoughts went back to those days in the convent, when I had asked the Lord to show me how to be crucified with Him, realising it would mean humiliation, degradation, self-denying, and dying to self. Had I really meant the Lord to carry it this far? I do not think I had meant it *quite* this way, but as I knew He was in it all with me, I knew I would not have changed my mind. With His grace, I *could* and *would* go through with it. I must have smiled at my thoughts, for a Simba came over to ask what I had to smile about?

The man in the room opposite came to, and began to moan and cry. We longed to go to him to help and comfort him, but we dared not move.

An officer came in and told us the fathers had been sentenced to death by the Colonel. When we heard machine-gun fire, we would know it was all over. The Colonel had said they were not to kill us yet, "So just relax and don't be afraid." Strange comfort!

Sister Fredeganda began to shake, and the nursing sister nearby said she was very hot. Then, and not until then, did we hear how just prior to entering chapel the previous evening, Sister had not felt well, and had taken her own temperature; it had been 104° F. She went to chapel, and was going to report sick afterwards, but was arrested beforehand. No wonder she had collapsed on our march to the prison-house, and no wonder she had looked so deathly pale during the night. Not a word of complaint all the time. Now she was in the throes of malarial chills. The guard fetched an officer, who somewhere found some quinine. Poor Sister, as though it was not enough being elderly and slightly infirm, and in prison under such circumstances — but to be so ill on top of it all!

We heard the noise of roll-call in the distance; we wondered what would happen next.

Some of the Congolese sisters at the convent arrived about 3 p.m. (all time from now on was judged by the sun). They had come with bread and butter, and some black coffee and sugar. The women were allowed to eat, and we ate hungrily. The men were not allowed a thing; the Simbas said they no longer had need. The Congolese sisters whispered that they had seen the fathers through the windows. They had been told of the sentence of death and were very calm and resigned. They added that they were worried about them. So were we. The sisters added, "For you, we have no fear, but for them there is no hope."

The bread finished, the Congolese sisters went back to the convent, and we returned to our prison-room.

Suddenly at about 4 p.m. we heard shouts, and people running, and somebody screaming hysterically, "Give them the command," followed by a loud cheer. My blood ran cold. The sisters did not know what the "command" was, but I knew it was the special Simba torture. It seemed as if my heart was trying to burst out of my chest, and going so rapidly and loudly, I was sure it could be heard.

The man in the room opposite was dragged out, and the Simba guards kept us informed with a running commentary. The priests were dragged out into the street and "the command" was administered. How they stood it is beyond any human comprehension. As the ropes were tightened on their legs and arms, making their bodies into a backward arch, one screamed, the first we had heard.

Some of the sisters were crying, but most were like marble statues, and their moving lips alone showed that they were indeed alive. They had known some of these men for years, in the course of their work and worship. Some of the men were old; two in particular were over seventy and had long white beards. Some were young, the youngest was only twenty-four, others in their late twenties and early thirties.

A truck pulled up, more beatings; the truck moved away, and shortly afterwards was silence, an uneasy silence. Our guard told us the men had been released from their bonds, stripped naked, and were being marched down to the river Rubi. How we prayed for those men; words are inadequate.

After a short while, more shouts, this time in the distance; then the rattle of machine-gun fire and we knew the thirty-one men were in eternity. The time was 5.30 p.m. The sisters surreptitiously crossed themselves. I asked the Lord to forgive the Simbas. Later we heard they had been lined up at the river, then called upon one by one, a stab into the left chest, when they fell, machetes to their necks. Any still living when they were in the water were given a *coup-de-grace* by Simbas in canoes, which explained the machine-gun fire we had heard.

The population of Buta, realising the enormity of the crime, fled to the forest. An unnatural silence fell on the town.

It must have been about 6.30 p.m. The light was on in our room, nobody had moved or spoken since the men had been shot about an hour previously. Suddenly the door opened, and before our horrified and sickened gaze, there stood a half-naked Simba. The perspiration was running down his body in rivulets. He held a dripping leg of a white man! It had been crudely severed at the knee. His long two-edged hunting knife was in his other hand, still bloody. I wanted to take my eyes off the leg, but could only stare at it, transfixed. Nobody in the room had moved, but we were each conscious of the reactions of the others.

He advanced into the room, still out of breath with running. He stood there, holding the leg for all to see clearly. He asked what it was, and not getting an answer, asked again, directing his question at me, as I was the nearest. My equilibrium quickly restored, I answered the obvious thing, "It is a white man's leg." Satisfied that it had been identified as *white*, he asked another sister what she thought of it; she calmly replied that the man was dead, and that this was only his body, and it didn't matter. He then thrust the leg into her hands, and made us all in turn hold it in two hands, even the children. Chantal asked her mother, "What is it?" And Madame answered "It is something they killed today," giving the impression it was an animal. The children were satisfied.

The man put the leg on the floor, and gave us a long talk on the fate of those who communicate with the National Army.

He went out, taking the leg with him, but leaving a bloody stain on the floor. We were glad we did not know to which father the leg belonged; to us it was just representative of them all.

Shortly afterwards an officer came in and stood in front of me, and asked where was Mademoiselle Margarita. It was Captain Jean-Pierre, the General's outrider. I identified myself; he had not recognised me without my glasses, regardless of the fact that I was one of the only two who did not wear the habit! He solemnly shook hands and then went out telling the guards to take care of me as I was a Protestant. I apologised to the sisters, adding that under the circumstances we were all in this together, regardless of religious beliefs. Later, when we had Catholic guards, the sisters were to apologise to me!

We were left alone for several hours. The guards said we could sleep if we wanted. They gave us some paper to put our heads upon, but a sheet of paper is a very poor pillow, and the hours we had sat through were a poor soporific for our troubled and saddened minds. We tossed and turned; only the children slept, and they fitfully. Some sisters wept quietly.

Some time before midnight, an officer came in with two mulattoes. They stared at us in simulated horror for our condition and surroundings. The officer said he had received orders from the Colonel to hide us in the forest until the National Army and the mercenaries had gone. "Don't worry," he added, "we won't let those barbarian National Army find you." We would have hugged a National Army man if he had shown up – barbarian or otherwise!

They left us to digest the full import of his words. To hide us in the forest! My heart sank! The only words which ran through my mind were, "But He knoweth the way that I take, when He hath tried me I shall come forth as gold" (Job 23 : 10). I had read this only a day or two before in my devotions, and then had asked the Lord to make me "as gold". Was this the way, the only way, I could be as gold? I silently accepted it as from His hand, not understanding, but believing it was somehow all caught up in His plan for my life.

The children wakened hungry. A sister had saved two crusts from our bread that afternoon and, dry as they were, the children ate them. We were all so grateful for the foresight of the sister.

A few minutes later we were ordered outside for our trek to the forest. The officer of the guard said it was 12.30 a.m.

9

Back to the Jungle

WE lined up outside our prison-house, and were counted. Satisfied, they put us in twos, the children being counted as one, and we set off for the march to the jungle.

It was a dark, moonless night, and I tripped several times as I could not see the holes and ridges in the road. The Superior, realising that five of us were half-blind without glasses, asked permission to rearrange the party, giving each of us a sister with good eyes to help us along. I was grateful. I can only describe it as being in a perpetual fog, straining one's eyes to see just a little further and not succeeding.

The Superior herself was suffering greatly with the pain in her back, and so was Sister Fredeganda who headed the procession and thus set the pace. Because of the fortitude of this sister, the Simbas were always very kind to her, and would let her go first in any walking we had to do.

We walked on past the now silent river, our hearts grieved at the brutality the men had suffered before being mercifully shot. We did not speak, each one busy with her own thoughts.

The road we took was called the Basali Trail, and ran alongside Buta, and at right angles to the main Stanleyville road.

The first stop was the hospital. A nursing sister was sent in to find blankets. She found three, and four small cot-sheets — we were nineteen in our party, seventeen women and two children. We then walked on and into the black night. In reality it was not far, maybe three miles at the most, but in the dark, with two sick sisters plus two children who were tired, and five women with impaired sight, it seemed a long way.

Eventually we arrived at a village and the first person we met was Patricia, the Colonel's latest wife whom he had abducted from the convent a month before and forced to renounce her vows. She had laid out mattresses, stolen from the convent, on the ground and thankfully we laid down our wearied bodies. The children fell asleep immediately. Patricia told us quietly that the Colonel had run away over the border — she believed it was to the Sudan — until the trouble died down. She said the time was 3.45 a.m.

We huddled together as best we could under the blankets and sheets. I realised then what a disadvantage it was to wear modern clothes and not the mediaeval clothes of a nun! My legs and feet were cold, as were my arms. Madame also complained of the cold — not out loud of course, just in my ear, we kept it between ourselves.

It was not long before it was morning and we arose and shook ourselves, and wondered what the day would bring. Was it really only thirty-six hours since we were first arrested? It seemed like weeks.

They gave us a handful of rice and a few half-ripe plantains, but apart from the children nobody was hungry. There was plenty of water, and we drank our fill thirstily. "In everything give thanks" — we thanked the Lord for the water and the warm sunshine, we asked for grace for a further day.

It was decided to walk us back to the hospital which was on the outskirts of the town. Our hopes went up a little. Maybe the mercenaries would find us after all! Maybe . . .

We arrived there about midday. Somebody came with several hot corn cobs which he had boiled for us; we had a quarter of one each. The children were given bananas. The nursing sisters were allowed to hunt for mattresses, and found three, two feet six inches wide and five feet long, and one inch thick; they also found four pillows. These we made quickly into beds for the two sick sisters, the Sister Superior who was in great pain by this time and looked pale, and Sister Fredeganda for whom they had found some anti-malarial drugs. We were glad when the sisters found some codeine tablets for the Sister Superior.

The guards were changed frequently, and according to their beliefs so they would harass us or otherwise.

The place was filthy; we had no option but to sit on the floor. Late in the afternoon, about 4.30, we heard a plane overhead; it was very low. The guards rushed in and shut the one window we had open. They were furious. They really believed we had communicated with it — why else would it fly right over the place where we were? We did not bother to answer him. We listened for bombs, but there were none. We knew then that the National Army would not bomb in case we were hit too.

As the sound of the plane died in the distance, we heard other ominous sounds. Blood-thirsty Simbas were outside, demanding our lives. Our guards somehow kept them at bay. I looked round the room; everybody was busy praying except me. I soon joined in! It was not that we were afraid to die, but we were afraid of *how* we would die. It is one thing to die in bed after an illness, or to be shot dead quickly, but knowing their brutality we were afraid of being speared to death, or slowly dismembered. Thoughts run riot under such circumstances, and it needed an S.O.S. in prayer to bring them under control again.

An officer came in, harangued us in Lingala and Swahili, and said we would die at his hand. He wielded his two-edged knife, and I recognised him as the man who had come in the previous evening with the severed leg. He said he would take the Sister Superior first and whereas the day before it had been a leg, today he would bring in her head, like they did to John the Baptist's head, only without the plate! He said he was going to call his men together to help him, and to set the guard on the bridge, and would be back in half an hour. In the meantime, he would have everybody's stockings or socks, whatever they wore. He took them out with him.

We sat in silence, then quietly the Superior said in French, so that both Madame and I could understand, "Today, sisters, we have not eaten, but never mind, tonight we will have supper with the Lord!"

If the sisters had anything in their hearts against another, it was confessed and forgiven openly. I thanked the Superior for her kindness to me, and all the sisters for their love. Madame did the same. The children were so different at this time. Ann sat unperturbed and ate a banana, but Chantal, who understood Lingala, whimpered, "But Mummy, I don't want to die yet." Her mother promised her that she would see her beloved papa and the little one was in a measure comforted.

Once again I had come to the place of facing death. There were no regrets, except maybe that of having given so little time to the Lord's service. Once again I prepared my soul to meet the Lord, and was at peace. I could not understand why He had allowed me to live through two massacres, and now would allow me to die. It did not make sense to me, but I knew He was Sovereign Lord and He never made a mistake. It is not necessary to understand all the "whys" and "wherefores" as long as we believe that He is Sovereign, for then everything falls into the right perspective.

Half an hour passed, an hour, darkness was falling, and the man did not come back. He had run away! We were left with four armed guards, and they too were alone with us. Everybody else had fled!

It rained hard that night, and next morning when we were lined up prior to leaving, we noticed a large puddle where the roof had leaked. We all knelt down, one by one, and washed our face and hands, drying them on our skirts or hankies. We left tide-marks enough to rejoice the heart of any boy, we were so filthy!

We set out, with Sister Fredeganda heading the file. We took with us the three blankets and three mattresses. I carried one mattress rolled up, tied around with the belt from my dress.

and it was carried on my shoulder. We walked approximately
four miles, and were then ushered into a small village, into a
tiny hut. The guards sat outside the door. Planes flew overhead. We tried to relax but it was so difficult. Near midday
somebody came with a large pot of boiled rice and some
bananas. We were ravenously hungry. As we began to eat, we
heard a hurried conversation going on outside our door
between the guard and someone who had just arrived. All the
Simbas had fled from Buta, and as far as military personnel
was concerned, the town was deserted. According to what we
could hear, the mercenaries had arrived at Buta, and were now
at the hospital searching for us, only four miles away.

The guard came in and peremptorily ordered us to get our
things together; we were to go further into the forest trail.

It was a hot, cloudless midday, the sun being directly overhead. We began the long walk. I shouldered one mattress and
followed. Our guards had now become eight.

If a plane was heard overhead, we were ordered to hide under
a tree, otherwise we had to keep on walking.

Having lost their socks or stockings, the sisters were unused to walking without them and consequently all had severe
multiple blisters. Madame was wearing a pair of sandals, which
were very fragile, and after three or four miles the straps broke.
My sandals were not in ideal condition but at least I was used
to walking in them and did not suffer blisters. We kept up a
steady pace all day and were very thirsty. With each step we
knew we were going further away from the mercenaries.

At last we came to a place where we could rest; the shadows
were long and down at the 6 p.m. position. We had been six
hours coming twelve miles!

Somebody in the village found us some native-type beds and
the sisters sank down wearily. They took off their shoes. Poor
dears! Blisters for most of them, including the children. One
sister was so weary she wept. Sister Superior and Sister
Fredeganda both smiled, but did not speak. Some fruit was

brought, and one of the nursing sisters divided it into nineteen portions. I had the privilege of taking it round the group as I was one of the few without a blister.

One of the men of the village prepared a small room for us, and also gave us water and soap with which to wash. It was only enough for a basinful each, but it felt so good on our dirty bodies it could have been a full bath!

Whilst the room was being prepared, a group of angry Simbas came, fleeing from Buta. They wanted to kill us, but our guards were able to control them and after stealing a few chickens they left us.

Thankfully we entered the room, which had been swept; we spread out the three mattresses and blankets, and having locked the door, after a short word of prayer, we lay down, but not to sleep. The floor was cold and hard, and we were overtired physically, mentally and emotionally.

Next morning at daybreak we had a handful of cold rice and a mug of piping-hot milkless and sugarless tea, but it tasted like nectar to me!

After half an hour we were on the road again. Several of the sisters had torn their dresses to make bandages for their feet, and thus bound we made but slow progress.

It was almost midday, and we had marched a further eight miles in six hours; we were tired, hot and thirsty. Suddenly, as we passed a group of houses, I heard "Mama Margarita, Mama Margarita!" I turned to look, but with my poor vision could not identify anybody. The owner of the voice came nearer, and taking my hand said again, "Mama Margarita". It was one of our U.F.M. evangelists called Ndimu Gaspar. The first Protestant I had met in over three months! I was so thrilled; at last there was somebody in the area who knew me. He asked me to stop and talk to him, but I hurriedly whispered that we were prisoners and not allowed to stop. He said he would follow and find out where we were going to stay.

We trudged on maybe another mile and were then told to

make our way into the next village. We were only too glad to comply. The sun was directly overhead and the sky was cloudless, we were thirsty and several of the sisters were having real pain from their numerous blisters.

They gave us a little mud hut and we all squeezed into it, thankful for the cool, and the opportunity to rest.

Several men came in, some of whom knew me from Bengamisa and Banalia. They were too far away for me to recognise them clearly.

The evangelist was as good as his word. After about an hour and a half he came back. He entered the hut without asking permission, and called for Mademoiselle Hayes. My full name! Very seldom do the Congolese use it, and here was one who seldom met me, using it correctly. He called "Yaka" (come), then as if in explanation to the sisters who were perturbed by his authoritative voice, he added, "It's all right, I am an evangelist and she is one of our missionaries." They were very impressed by his charming manner.

Bless his heart, he had brought a large bowl of hot sweet potatoes and a three-pound tin of powdered milk; the latter, which was an exorbitant price, had probably been hoarded for a "rainy day". He gave it all freely, and then proceeded to give me news of the other evangelists. He reassured me that Bo Martin was alive, and also Masini Phillipe of Bongondza.

He was holding services in his little village church every day; not many came any more, but up to then he had continued his work faithfully.

The next time he came he asked why I was having trouble with my eyes, and when it was explained to him that the Simbas had taken my glasses without hesitation he brought his out from his pocket and offered them to me. I was very touched by this magnificent gesture, for to own a pair of glasses was to a Congolese practically a status symbol, and I knew he had bought them fairly recently. The sisters were most impressed by his generosity, and it could have been a real temptation to bask in reflected glory, but I humbly gave thanks to the Lord for such a dedicated personality as Ndimu Gaspar.

He pointed out one of the Simba guards and whispered that he too was supposedly a believer. Later I understood why he said "supposedly", as he was the cruellest of them all. Actually when I asked him if he had ever believed, he quoted several scriptures to me, then told me to shut up as he did not want to talk about religion. His name was Pascal.

Several villagers came to see us and brought gifts of fruit and vegetables, for which we were grateful.

The Simbas gave us permission to collect some leaves to put on the floor so that we could lie down at night.

We had water with which to wash, and somebody gave us soap, and two of the sisters were allowed down to the river with some clothes to wash. There was nothing to do except draw pictures in the sand to amuse the children. We took it in turns to walk up and down to pray.

We heard that Buta had fallen, and that the mercenaries were on their way to us.

For three nights we stayed in the little hut; during the third night our guards came in and unearthed the things they had stolen and subsequently buried. One guard, Alexis, said that the mercenaries were only a few miles away, but that the Simbas had felled trees and this had effectually impeded their progress. He thought they would be along by 8 a.m., in which case the Simbas would take flight and leave us to be found.

Alas! The Simba named Pascal was the leader of our guards and he refused to comply with this line of thought. He emphasised that the Colonel had given orders that the sisters were to be surrendered to him alive and well and *not* to the mercenaries. Therefore we would move at dawn. The others had to agree.

During the small hours of the morning a mob came demanding our lives, and Alexis, the young guard, was able to prevent them breaking down the door. Inside the house, half of the sisters formed a human barricade to the door, and the rest of us prayed urgently for help. The Lord answered prayer rapidly, for as suddenly as they had come, they decided to go. As they moved away we heard them threatening to destroy the bridge nearest to us.

Finally the guard, Alexis, called to us to relax as the Simbas had gone. We lay down again, our thoughts in a whirl.

It was during this time that the thoughts of writing this book materialised, and as we lay waiting for the dawn, and as we hoped for liberation, I mentally made notes and even had chapter headings decided.

Dawn came, we anticipated early deliverance, but Pascal was adamant. We all tried to explain how simple it would be to leave us in the hut, and for them to flee whilst they had time and, apart from Pascal, the Simbas were with us. We cajoled, promised, and pleaded; he would not budge, and eventually tiring of our perpetual demands, curtly ordered us to pack our few belongings and march directly into the jungle, at right-angles to the road. We were powerless to do anything but obey.

It is hard to describe our feelings as we left in single file down the narrow track. Once more our hopes had been raised only to be dashed down again. Almost mechanically we walked, sharing the loads between us. After ten minutes we came to a shallow river. Taking off our shoes we waded through it, and then kept our shoes off to wade through mud on the other side.

Exactly which direction we went is hard to tell, as the jungle is all confusion to us white people. Alexis led the procession, and eventually brought us out to a small clearing, where there was a little leaf shelter. The clearing was small, and the trees tall and thick, so the sun did not penetrate, and it was cold and damp.

Once there, the Simbas made us sit on the ground in a group. They shouted and raved at us. Alexis, who previously had been so nice to us, now became vicious. We were not allowed to speak. They decided they would take us one by one into the forest. We refused to go; they tried to make one sister go, but she struggled and so much noise ensued, they decided to leave us alone for fear the mercenaries should hear.

We heard later that the mercenaries reached the hut where we had slept just a few hours after we had left.

The Simbas worked hard to complete our shelter for the night. They went back to the village and brought two African-type beds of wooden slats on a frame. At least they were off the ground, and whoever lay on them would not need a mattress.

That night it rained. The roof leaked badly. We readjusted ourselves. Fourteen could lie down, and five sat up crouched in a small space. We were very cold, and took it in turns to lie down. Neither way was very comfortable. Once again the long robes of the sisters proved more utilitarian than my modern dress. They could wrap up their feet and their arms were covered whilst mine were exposed to both cold and mosquitoes. Day dawned, and we each had a piece of cold manioc to eat and a quarter of a ripe plantain. We sat huddled together for warmth, whilst others lay down and tried to rest. The day passed slowly.

We laughed at how filthy we were. The sisters' white robes were stained and torn. We were unwashed and unkempt; at least Madame and I were unkempt, as we could not comb our hair. During the day we experimented with wet leaves for washing our faces and hands. If they did not remove the dirt, at least we *felt* fresher.

That night we again took it in turns to lie down, and it did not rain which did help the situation.

Prayer under these circumstances tended to become very self-centred; all we could see was our own particular need and also concentration was difficult.

Sunday morning dawned bright and clear, and we reminded

each other it was the feast of Pentecost, or Whitsun. Laughingly, we bade each other a happy day! Pentecost! The day when the disciples were filled with the Holy Spirit and were able to preach in a diversity of tongues. Here we were, representing four European languages, Dutch, Flemish, French and English, we all knew Lingala, and I knew some Swahili also. Several sisters knew the tribal tongue of their particular territory, and yet our mouths were closed! Our guards represented four tribes, but we were not allowed to speak to each other save in a whisper let alone to them. As we pondered on these facts we wondered why it had been necessary for us to pass through this particular lesson.

As I pondered on the feast of Pentecost, I remembered again that I had asked the Lord to be rescued by Pentecost. So far all the feast days of the Christian Church had gone by, from Christmas, the birth of the Lord, right through His trial, crucifixion, burial and resurrection, on through His ascension into Heaven, and now we were at the place where He had sent the Holy Spirit in His place.

Why had not the Lord answered prayer? I had prayed believing as commanded in the Word of God. Then it was as I thus meditated, that I realised I was asking for liberation in *my* time, in *my* way. *I* had it all nicely planned out and wanted God to do *my* will, forgetting that I had prayed so often, "Not my will but *Thine* be done."

Humbly I acknowledged my egotism in this, and then told the Lord I was willing to be a prisoner as long as He required it of me, provided He would grant the necessary grace to go through each day. As I prayed I was conscious of the burden being lifted and my peace was complete once again.

The guards were cold and wet, and decided we could not stay where we were, but must go to a place which had a more adequate shelter and plenty of warm sunshine. Once again we picked up our paltry belongings, and following the guards through more forest and finally to a very large clearing, entered a cultivated "garden", which was more like a field in size.

At last we were in the warm sunshine! Quickly we thawed out. Wood for a fire was brought by a Simba, and as we had some corn and plantains, we cooked over the open fire.

Somewhere during our travels we had acquired two cooking pots, one serving spoon, two aluminium plates, and two hub-caps, one off a car and one off a motor-cycle; these latter made excellent deep plates for three people at a time. For those without plates we used leaves, which when properly folded were quite good for everything except soup. We ate with our fingers.

For washing-up we used the water with which we had boiled the corn; if the pot needed scouring, it was quite a simple matter to take a handful of grass, rub it in the soil and the pot would soon be clean. There was no need to dry our "dishes"; the sun did that for us.

We also possessed a plastic bucket and a beaker. It was strange, but when the bucket was full of water nobody was thirsty, but as soon as it was empty we were all gasping for a drink. The sisters who could see clearly would take it in turns to go to the river for water.

One problem we had which was quite distressing was feeding the children. The food we had was inadequate and not very filling, and now that the tension had lessened somewhat, both children developed voracious appetites. In fact we were all terribly hungry, but of course, as adults, understanding the situation, we did not complain. So to hear the children crying with hunger and not to have anything really nutritious to give them was upsetting. The Simbas gave them bananas, and young Ann ate so many she had an upset tummy for days afterwards.

That Sunday evening the Simbas proudly led us across the field to a place they had spent most of the day building. It was a long low hut, with bunk-like shelves made with tree-bark, about three feet off the floor. The sides were open, but later two walls of bark were added at the far end and along half the length of the back. The two wooden beds were added. It was more comfortable than the previous one inasmuch as there was room for us *all* to lie down, but we were so tightly packed it was like a hen-house!

I was given a place between the Sister Superior on my right, who was now very much better, and a Mother Superior of another order on my left. Our feet dangled over the end. For me it was not too bad, but some of the sisters were tall, and their feet and legs were without support. When we went to lie down at night—always at sundown—we would each one wriggle into position; there was no room to curl up. It used to be amusing, for if one turned to the left, then one by one, like an advancing wave, we would all turn to the left, or vice versa.

The bunks were hard, and as we became thinner they seemed even harder. We would gather dead leaves and make mounds upon which we would lie, but always by morning they would be scattered. None of us slept very much, it was always too cold and hard.

For the most part the Simbas would leave us undisturbed once we had lain down at night, and it was at this time the discipline of the sisters was so helpful. Used as they were to being quiet at bedtime, we would automatically, as with mutual consent, stop talking as soon as the last person had lain down. Then it was we could really pray undisturbed. I would see the sisters cross themselves, and see their hands folded and know they were communing with the Lord. It was a very blessed time for us all, a time when we were able to catch up with ourselves, to be able to lose ourselves in communion.

For me, I would go over various aspects of the Lord's earthly life, and would afterwards find a parallel in the life we were living, and from that derive comfort. The Lord had gone before, He understood how we felt. He too had experienced the discomforts of a nomadic life whilst He was preaching.

One day we had a visit from the owner of the garden where we were staying. He turned out to be a U.F.M. church member.

The evangelist, Ndimu Gaspar, had told him about me, and he had come now to find me and to talk to me. He asked if I had a Bible, and I answered in the negative.

A few days later he came back and brought word from Ndimu that he had fled with his family to his own garden several miles in the forest in the opposite direction to us. Ndimu had sent in a small copy of *The Way of Salvation*, a Scripture Gift Mission booklet in Lingala. We were all very grateful for this, and we read it in turns, including some of the Simba guards. I was very moved by such fidelity, the more so when we were surrounded by men who were unlovely and cruel in the extreme.

We adopted a routine for each day. Rising at dawn, a sister would light the fire, while others would go together to find the leaves to make soup, or *pondu*, a Congolese vegetable much like spinach. As I could not see very well to gather these leaves and my sandals were not in good condition, I stayed back and tidied the hut generally, and swept both the inside and the surrounds. The "broom" was a bunch of unripe rice.

When the sisters returned with the leaves and whatever else they could find – sometimes they found a few tomatoes – we would all work together to prepare the food. The villagers were compelled to bring manioc – a root vegetable not unlike potato when cooked, and plantains. Peanuts were given from time to time, corn and the occasional onion. These foods take a lot of preparation, and we would spend several hours a day peeling, cutting, pounding or just stirring. About 9 a.m. we would stop work and eat cold manioc left over from the previous evening, and bananas, washed down with water. Once somebody brought some coffee grains, and we roasted them, pounded them and finally made a brew of coffee. We lacked sugar and milk so drank it without, but once we had been given honey so we used that!

The Simbas were ashamed of our filthiness, and from somewhere produced a large box of soap. They said we had to wash ourselves and our clothes. Accordingly, they took a party of five sisters to the river. As we did not have a change of clothing, it became quite a matter of ingenuity as to which garment was washed first. The sisters whose turn it was to have their dresses washed would stay in the hut all day whilst they dried. The Simbas insisted on accompanying us to the river, so we did not feel free to bathe, and would just wash our hands, faces and feet. Not everybody would be allowed to go on the same day, and I seldom went because of the difficulty of seeing my way through the dark jungle. I did go on three occasions on my own with a Simba; this was just to fill a bucket with water. Each time I tripped and stumbled so badly that he finally had to carry the bucket of water and guide me by the hand. My ablutions therefore were confined to a small basin, rather the size of a sugar bowl. It is amazing how much one can wash with so little!

At midday we would eat whatever had been prepared, and then I was able to help with the "washing-up" previously mentioned.

This was followed by a so-called siesta; the sun being directly overhead, and our hut so low, there were no shadows, and we would lie on our bunks until 2 or 2.30 p.m. when the shadows would be long enough to afford protection.

Afternoons were spent much as the mornings, in preparing food, keeping the fire going, getting water, and keeping the place swept and tidy.

At approximately 5.30 we would eat our evening meal, saving enough manioc or plantains for next day's breakfast. We found that no matter how much we ate, we were always ravenously hungry after an hour or two. Again the children suffered more than us in this respect. They were not used to African food, and at first would hardly touch it, but later would eat and eat and still complain of hunger after a short while.

Just at sundown the others would all congregate to watch the monkeys in the treetops, as they made their way home each evening. The "ooh's" and "aah's" of everybody would tell me that the monkeys were seen clearly. Unhappily, with my defective sight I did not see them once. The children of course, were absolutely delighted.

Like the monkeys, we retired to rest as daylight faded. Each night Chantal would ask "Mummy, is this our last night here?" and always Madame would answer, "Perhaps, only the Lord knows."

In our day's programme I have not mentioned prayer or Bible reading. We did not have a Bible, and we could not organise times for prayer. The Simbas would be furious if they caught a sister crossing herself or praying. So we each one had to find a way and time for devotions without bringing it to their notice. For myself, and I know for several others too, I would walk round and round the hut, usually with my hands behind my back. I found, too, it helped in concentration to walk. We were all finding it increasingly difficult to concentrate for long periods, and this way the movement of the body liberated the mind for prayer. I suppose it was because when we were seated we were so uncomfortable that we were distracted. We sat either on the ground or on a low tree-trunk, or else in the hut on the bunk.

We would discuss amongst ourselves our situation. One day we heard the Simbas talking and they said the mercenaries had gone back to Buta and had given up the search. We were very despondent. Yet we could not correlate this to the fact that God would never abandon us. "Lo, I am with thee to deliver thee"; "I will be with thee even unto the end of the world". We had these promises, and these we firmly believed; nothing could shake our faith in God. Looking at the situation in the purely human realm, it seemed as though there was no more hope, and we felt we had been abandoned. We would comfort each other with the Lord's promises, and count ourselves privileged to have been allowed to tread this particular path-way. Our times were in *His* hands, and nobody could alter His plans for us. We knew that when it was the right moment we would be liberated, not a moment too early nor too late.

During these days and weeks, the Simbas who guarded us were nine in number. Several would be out on patrol in the daytime, but we were never left without a guard. We were not allowed to speak out loud, and they did not like to see more than three of us talking together. Several times they heaped indignities upon us. Nothing much maybe – to walk without shoes for several hours; to be lined up, or sat in a row on the muddy ground whilst they berated us. On occasions they would pull somebody's nose – funny in retrospect maybe, but very painful and humiliating for the recipient at the time.

Twice a plane flew overhead, a small twin-engined plane, flying fairly low. We were not allowed to speak, indeed we dared not show any interest at all in it. Afterwards we would be accused of having been in contact with it, and were threatened with death. Since our release we have learned that there were two flights *a day* to Buta the entire time, yet in the Lord's providence, they chose a route away from us.

We were told by the guards that we would never be found by the white people, as they did not know the jungle and therefore would not be able to penetrate very far; but they also added that at the first intimation of the white people coming near, we would be killed. We knew this was no idle threat.

Imagine too, the mental agony of Madame Le Gros; the Simbas often said that when they killed us they would spare the two children and take them to live with them in their villages. In fact two of them went so far as to decide which child each would take.

The sanitary arrangements for us were appalling. The Simbas cleared a small area, but so arranged it that there was no privacy whatsoever. As far as possible, we would try and arrange it that one or two sisters would "happen" to be standing together talking just in the place where we would be effectively screened.

Because of our modest washing habits, one of the Simbas

really thought we did not know how to bathe, and asked me one day if white people *never* wash all over! I refrained from explaining why we did not, as this would have made them more insistent than ever. However he brought a bucket of water, and calling us together began to demonstrate how to wash all over. We tactfully withheld our grins until he had gone.

The villagers who brought the food, and incidentally they were not paid, were always in trouble because they had not brought enough or what they had brought was not good quality. On one such occasion we were lying down during siesta-time and heard the arguments as usual, when suddenly we heard the word "command", and accompanied by the cries and groans of the poor fellow, they tied him up in their barbarous way, feet to elbows.

At this point we were ordered out of the hut to watch the spectacle. Madame and the children were allowed to stay back.

The poor fellow was on his side, and at his mouth was a small unpeeled manioc, several palm-nuts, and a raw unpeeled plantain. By means of his spear, the Simba made the man eat them all, earth and peel as well. When he had finished, they untied him, and made him drink a large bowl of water. By the time he was through, his stomach stuck out from his abdomen, like a large displaced hernia. Following this, to our amazement, the Simbas then shook hands with him and invited him to sit with them in their hut for a while and they chatted and laughed together like bosom pals!

The last Monday we were in the jungle Alexis and two other Simbas went out on patrol, and at 4 p.m. came back, each with a new machine-gun and ammunition. They had robbed a fellow Simba. That night they sat handling their spoil and regaling each other with accounts of the wonderful acts of bravery they were going to perform.

On the Tuesday they went out on patrol, now suitably armed, and when they came back they were minus guns. The

Commander had taken them, and the boys were duly punished that day with their own "command" treatment.

On Wednesday we had a letter from the Commander, written in pencil, saying in effect, "We know you are trying to contact your white relatives" (meaning the mercenaries of course) "but you will not succeed. We do not want to hear of any more trouble from your camp. You are our prisoners and you will obey your Simbas—or else. Remember this, if one Simba is shot in an attack, you will all die."

We felt this was, in essence, our death sentence, as we could not visualise our liberation without prior attack in the villages.

The Sister Superior said we must from now on live as though each hour was our last.

On Thursday it was chilly and drizzling so we stayed in the hut. The sisters sat along each of the bunks, and I was behind them. Suddenly I felt the desire to pray for deliverance, and as I lay down behind them they, realising I was praying, drew closer to shield me from the prying eyes of the Simbas.

As I prayed I was conscious of the overwhelming Presence of God, and even as I asked for a word from Himself, the text from Mark 5: 36, "Be not afraid, only believe", came to my conscious mind, and I knew with renewed assurance that the Lord had everything in hand.

On Friday the Simbas were restless. Up to this time we had always had adequate food, and always there was enough left over for the next meal. Now our supplies were running low, and they had heard that the villagers did not wish to supply any more. They talked amongst themselves about moving us to another place.

That night as we laid down to rest, I felt very burdened, in spite of the assurance of the day before. I argued with the Lord, and showed Him again how precarious our lives were. Again I reaffirmed my faith in Him and His word, but I remember so clearly saying to Him, "Lord, we are at the end of our tether, we cannot go on much longer under these conditions. Please burden the folk at home to pray; we are so tired and battered mentally, we cannot see our way clear to pray for ourselves." Again the words of the previous day came back, "Do not fear, only believe."

It rained in torrents all that night, and the roof leaked like a sieve. I was soaked, and was cold and miserable; my feet, rarely warm at the best of times, were so cold they were painful. None of us slept that night, and I am afraid I fidgeted quite a bit. One Superior next to me arranged her skirt so that it covered my legs, and the one on the other side arranged her veil to cover my shoulders.

So was spent our last night in captivity, though we did not realise it at the time.

IO

Rescued!

SATURDAY morning, June 26th, was cloudy, cold and damp. As we began to stir ourselves, word went round that vehicles had been heard on the road. Two of the sisters and Madame had heard them very early, almost before daybreak. Obviously the Simbas had, too, as they thought it was probably the National Army coming out to the villages for food for Buta.

The morning passed like all the others, save maybe we had all had a bad night and were more than usually tense after hearing about the trucks.

Our Simbas went on patrol again; at least they said that was where they were going. The sun came out during the morning and we felt warmer and a little more happy. Once or twice comments had been made about the possibility of the trucks being those of the mercenaries, when one of our guards came back having had a hair cut.

To cut their hair takes time, anything up to an hour, and we felt that he would not have had it done if the mercenaries were in the vicinity. If anybody would know who had driven the trucks, they would, as the grapevine system was near-perfect for communications, so we reasoned amongst ourselves.

We therefore dismissed any idea of rescue, and concentrated on the job in hand, preparing the midday meal. We peeled and pounded. But for the first time *there was nothing left for the next meal!*

Having eaten, we retired as usual for our siesta. Several villagers came and the Simbas demanded food from them.

Then they began to argue amongst themselves as to what they were going to do with us. As they argued the voices became louder and louder.

Because of their aggressiveness we stayed in the hut until 2.30 p.m.

Madame was on her way out of the hut at one end, and one sister was just putting her head out at the side. The Superior lying next to me had sat up, thus giving me an uninterrupted view out of the hut. The time was 2.31 p.m.

Suddenly the air was rent with shrieks and yells, *"Tirez, tirez"* (shoot, shoot), and machine guns spurted bullets. At the same time I saw white legs, indistinctly but white for all that — coming over the hilltop and down to us. Bullets whistled, the noise was terrifying. One Superior called out, "Don't shoot, don't shoot!" The sister who was almost out of the hut jumped back saying, *"C'est les blancs, c'est les blancs!"* (it is the white people). We held our breath. Little Chantal had thrown herself under the African-type bed, and during a lull in the gunfire, a white, unshaven, bespectacled face peered down under the roof and said with a cheerful grin, *"Bonjour mes soeurs, bonjour mesdames, venez, vous êtes liberées."* (Goodday sisters, goodday madames, come, you are liberated). Like the unpredictable females that we were we all burst into tears! The time was 2.35 p.m.

We jumped off our bunk, and streamed outside and there were our liberators! A crowd of tired, bearded, dirty but such happy men! We all shook hands, and tearfully said our "thank-you's". The one with spectacles who had first seen us was the Catholic chaplain and he was accompanied by the doctor.

They sought out Madame to tell her the wonderful news that her husband was out on the road waiting for her. It made our joy complete!

Without a backward glance to the hut, we immediately set off through the forest.

181

Of the four Simbas who had been there, three had been wounded, and one escaped. We passed the body of somebody who had been fatally injured, jerking his legs in the last throes of death.

As we walked away the mercenaries fired three mortar bombs, which was the signal to the others that we had been found, and they would thus all make their way back to the trucks.

After the brutality of the Simbas, it was wonderful to meet these gallant men. They surrounded us, some walking backwards in order to protect us on the walk back. Neither the doctor nor the chaplain were armed, though both were in camouflage clothes.

One of the sisters led me through the forest, through the river, now very much higher, and out on to the road. There was an empty house, and we all went in and ate the mercenaries' biscuits and drank their wonderful cold coffee!

The reader can imagine how our tongues were loosened! Somebody was despatched to find a bicycle for Sister Fredeganda, as the trucks were three or four miles down the road, the other side of the destroyed bridge.

The mercenaries had found a man to guide them to us, and we thanked him profusely. He asked to return with us, as he feared reprisals from the Simbas. His request was granted.

The bicycle arrived, and we set out once more, this time without fatigue; never have three miles seemed so short! We saw the large trees which had been felled across the road, and were quickly helped over.

Down the road were a group of mercenaries, and one detached himself from the rest and came running, arms held out; it was Monsieur Le Gros, and for a long minute Madame disappeared in his embrace. We were complete as a family . . .

The first jeep we met was named "Maggie" and all the sisters laughed and said it was mine. With a jeep so named, we *had* to be rescued.

We clambered on board a covered truck, with Sister Frede-ganda in the cabin. We talked, we prayed, and we wept together. We pinched each other to know if it was really true. Monsieur sat with Chantal on his lap, and his free arm round Madame; Ann sat with her mother. It made a beautiful picture.

Shortly before arriving at Buta we ran into another ambush. A tree had been felled that day across the road. The trucks stopped, the mercenaries jumped out, leaving the doctor and the chaplain with us. Monsieur Le Gros also jumped out, but was soon sent back to the cover of the truck; they were not going to risk losing him now!

It was not long before the convoy set off again. As we neared the bridge at Buta we became silent, remembering the thirty-one men who had died there just four weeks previously.

There was a hole in the canvas near me, and three of us peered out all along. The driver tooted all the way once we were in the town, and we stuck our white arms out of the hole; the people came running, just like following the pied piper.

In no time we were at the convent and surrounded by laugh-ing and crying Congolese. There were six Congolese sisters and two priests, and a brother, then the population. What a welcome!

The Congolese flag was flying, the quadrangle was full of military trucks, and mercenaries and National Army were all over the place.

We went in to see the Commander of the entire operation. He was so moved he could hardly speak. He took our proffered hands in both of his.

We then went to the chapel, and each one offered up her praise to the Lord in her own way. One could hear the sniffs all over the place. The chaplain and Monsieur Le Gros joined us.

Afterwards we made our way to the refectory, and saw a

table already prepared for nineteen! They had kept it laid the entire month, in faith believing they would find us.

Whilst we were eating, the chaplain lent me his spectacles (he was short-sighted too) to see all the sisters clearly. There they sat, in their indescribably filthy clothes, with such radiant happy faces. I returned the glasses sublimely content.

The next obvious thing to do was to clean up. There was an abundant supply of hot water, soap and towels. We went to see if our cases were still intact. Everybody else's was there, *except mine!* I did find one dress, my good sandals, and – oh precious find – my spare pair of spectacles! While I was ironing my dress, the Congolese Mother Superior came and took the iron out of my hand and said she wanted to do it for me. I let her – I knew how she felt.

We washed, combed and dressed, the sisters providing what I lacked in the way of other clothes.

The mercenaries stood around looking for all the world like the cat who had just stolen the cream. They had reason to be content!

One by one we made our way back to the chapel where the chaplain held a service of thanksgiving.

Surely this was the Lord's doing and was marvellous in our eyes. We gave Him all the praise. He had brought us through the fiery trial unharmed. Deuteronomy 8 was so apt, "And thou shalt remember all the way the Lord thy God led thee . . . in the wilderness, to humble thee, and to prove thee, to know what was in thine heart, whether thou wouldest keep His commandments or no. And He humbled thee, and suffered thee to hunger, and fed thee with manna which thou knewest not . . . that He might make thee know that man shall not live by bread alone, but by every word that proceedeth out of the mouth of the Lord . . ."

Once more we ate, and then on to bed. The Congolese sisters had moved out in order that we could have their beds. The mercenaries were in the other part of the convent.

None of us slept. One sister vomited all night, one or two wept, the rest of us tossed and turned, but at least the bed was comfortable, and we had pillows and blankets.

During that first evening a radio message had been sent through to Stanleyville, asking for planes to take us out of Buta. That must have been one of the happiest moments of the Commander's life!

11

Home-coming

SUNDAY dawned fine and clear.

Emotionally we were divided. We hated the thought of leaving Congo, our adopted land, leaving the friends we had made to the mercy of the Simbas, yet we knew there was little we could do to help them; rather we were an embarrassment. Our ordered lives had been uprooted. For the sisters the convent was in confusion; for me, I could not see any other way but to leave.

This was the land to which we had each one been individually called for service, and due to causes outside our control, we were going to have to leave. It hurt terribly. We love these people and they have become our brothers and sisters.

We went to the chapel to pray. It was a relief to place the burden in God's hands, knowing He had taken over the responsibility of running our lives for us. It is at times like these when we need to step out in faith, not seeing clearly the way, but believing that all things work together for good for those who are the called of God (Romans 8 : 28).

A mercenary gave me a khaki knapsack, and I packed into it my very few possessions. In taking my valise, the rebels had spurned one or two personal effects and these, plus a handbag we had found, were all I possessed.

It was about this time I began worrying about *how* I was going to enter the homeland again. I had no money, no passport and no papers to prove my identity or nationality. I wondered if there would be time in Leopoldville to contact the Embassy to ask for a paper to say I was British. I hoped I could borrow some money for the phone call. If there was no time in Leopoldville, would I be able to convince the authorities in Belgium? So I worried. Why it did not occur to me that the Lord Who had arranged our rescue in such a miraculous way, could surely be trusted to finish the job of getting me home to England, I do not know. All I know is I worried about it.

A plane and a helicopter were dispatched from Stanleyville. The helicopter never arrived. It was shot down by the rebels.

Half of our number went in the plane, and the other half went back to the convent to await a further plane. I was with the latter group.

They gave us an enormous lunch, but we were really too excited and emotionally over-wrought to do full justice to the meal. At 2.30 p.m. we heard a plane in the distance. We jumped into the back of a truck, and in eight minutes were at the little airstrip. We were reminded that we were still in enemy-infested territory as we saw the sandbags and mounted machine-guns manned all along the runway.

A last wave to the mercenaries, we were strapped in, the engines started, and in next to no time we were off. The plane circled Buta, and flew fairly low over the convent; it was a kind gesture from the pilot but a poignant moment for the sisters.

We flew on and on, over forest, broken here and there by a red-ribbon road or a small river. We sighted the River Aruwimi and I knew we were over Banalia territory. I crouched by the window and whispered adieus to all my loved ones there still hiding in the forest. I was not ashamed of the tears on my face.

Stanleyville! Eagerly we peered out; it looked just the same except that the market place was deserted. I do not know what we expected to see, but it all looked so normal.

We touched down, and a group of priests came to greet us across the tarmac. There were two U.S. Army soldiers, and I went to greet them in English. They knew who I was and had messages for me from folks in Leopoldville. A young civil engineer from Lancashire was working in Stanleyville; he too had permission to come and to greet me. We did not know each other, though he knew more about me than I did about him. Even now I do not recollect his name. I was very touched with his gesture of friendliness as the only British man in Stanleyville greeting the lone Briton just rescued.

Cars came, and we all squeezed in and were taken to Colonel Mulamba's (of the National Army) residence in Stanleyville. Here we had a wonderful reception. We met with the other half of our number who had left in the morning. Champagne was served all round, though I personally did not partake. Photographs, vaccinations, speaking English, French, Bangala, it was a delightful confusion.

An hour later, back to the airport. Together with other civilians we boarded the plane for Leopoldville. We were all so excited, none of us could think coherently.

Several priests came on the plane with us, and showed us newspapers and magazines telling of the deaths of the thirty-one men in May. I talked long with a priest who was of the same order as the Rev. Hermann Bischoff who had died at Banalia. On board were two men from the Protestant University of Stanleyville; one was Congolese, the other American. We talked a long time. In the multiplicity of names, I have forgotten theirs.

Leopoldville! We were all told to keep our seats until the hostess called us. The minutes seemed interminable. At last, "All the sisters from Buta to leave first, please," came the order. As we appeared on the gangway we heard the cheers and applause of those waiting to greet us.

The tarmac was seething with nuns, priests, Embassy staff, Protestant missionaries and reporters! Why had I worried about getting home? I was surrounded by English folk, Consular staff were there, Miss Jenkins of the Baptist Missionary Society greeted me with a hug. Mr. Drake, Field Leader of the B.M.S., was there, and newspaper reporters, and TV —

such a confusion of names, explanations and handshakes.

It was decided that I should go to the home of Mr. and Mrs. Drake, and so I bade farewell to my beloved Catholic sisters. They were taken to a convent in Leopoldville.

There were four priests who were going home to Europe that evening on vacation; they all gave up their seats to Monsieur and Madame Le Gros and the two children, and thus they were able to leave Congo but forty-five minutes after arriving in Leopoldville. It was a very gracious gesture on the part of the priests, and we were all grateful to them.

Mr. and Mrs. Drake did not spare any aspect of hospitality. A luxurious long soak in a hot bath, clean clothes, beautiful soothing music, delicious food and wonderful fellowship. Staying with them was like being in an oasis in the middle of a desert of confusion. There were no crowds, no noise, no tension. I will remain eternally grateful to them for their kindness.

It was here that I first heard that President Johnson had been elected. We were arrested in November, the day the election began in America. Mary Baker never did know who was the new President. News of my parents was given me, and I rejoiced to know they were both alive and well. They had suffered much on my behalf.

The names of all those of our mission who had died were told me, and I was shocked and saddened. I realised more than ever that my deliverance was a miracle. Two copies of my own obituary, were given me – people say the nicest things!

At a press conference at the Consulate, everybody was most kind. I was given an emergency passport, and a ticket home; to think I had worried about it all! The Consulate staff were wonderful.

On Tuesday at midday I boarded a plane bound for Europe. The sisters had left at 8.30 a.m. that day. I found my seat. The lady next to me had a newspaper, and in it was an account of our rescue. As she read it she turned to me and said, "You boarded this plane in Congo, and this woman was in Leopold-ville; have you by any chance met her?" "This woman" was myself! I laughed and changed the subject. But my news had preceded me in any case.

The *Daily Express* had sent out a reporter and he travelled back with me and very kindly looked after me on the plane.

Paris! We touched down at 8.30 p.m. Although it was summer, I was cold and was glad of the heavy coat given me in Leopoldville. We tried to avoid meeting the press and their battery of cameras; as well try to prevent a fish from swim-ming. With them, to my immense joy, was the Rev. H. Jenkin-son, affectionately known as Kinso, the most senior missionary of U.F.M. in Congo. As I tried to avoid the onrush of cameras, Kinso called out, "Hi, Maggie, aren't you going to say hello?" I turned to face the owner of this wonderful voice, and the press closed in!

Another press conference, with its endless questions and photographs. Then at long last all went to catch their plane to London, and left Kinso and me in peace and quiet.

Only two days before I had heard he was alive, as the rebels had told me he was dead. Here he was, very much alive, and precious were those few moments with him as we exchanged news of those whom we loved. It was a relief to unburden to Kinso, as he knew so well the background to it all.

One more plane and an hour later we were at London Airport. Again the press, as well as the men from Scotland Yard, and that wonderful invention England has perfected, the London "Bobby".

Past the press and there in a group were various members of my family. Words are inadequate to describe that meeting. I will not even try.

Yet another press conference, and as I entered the room, more friends, from my church in London and from the Mission.

The press conference over, the family had their cars fairly

near, and here I would like to say how wonderfully kind and understanding were the airport authorities in all they did to make my homecoming such an unforgettable occasion.

As we drove away from the airport, there were two police outriders part of the way. Maybe it was as well, as it prevented my brother from speeding.

Home! My mother at the door, very much older and thinner, and looking very tired. My father looking very well, though now lame due to an accident two years before. I did not even know he had to walk with a stick until then. More brothers and sisters. Everybody talking at once.

It was 4.30 a.m. when I finally went to bed, but at 7.30 a.m. my sister came in to call me and dumped on my bed a beautiful chubby eighteen-month-old niece I had never seen before. She was more interested in my tea than me.

It was several days later, when I had opportunity of reading *Daily Light* again, that I read back to the evening portion of June 26th. It said, "It is a night to be much observed unto the Lord for bringing them out from the land of Egypt" (Exodus 12: 42). How appropriate it was!

How can one describe the innumerable emotions the following day, Thursday, when I entered the church in East London which I love so much? To meet Pastor Paul Tucker and friends again. To hear the testimonies of those who never gave up hope, and who continued to pray all the way through, was thrilling. I saw how the Lord had answered prayer over and above all I had dared to ask or think.

Since my rescue, we have heard from our Congolese brethren, and all the people from the village of Bopepe, including Pastor Bo Martin and his brother Pastor Asani are alive and well and safe.

But Pastor Phillipe Masini at the time of writing is still in rebel held territory with his son. The rebels, hearing that Bo Martin and others have been liberated, are now persecuting ie Christians. They have stood much this past year, and they need our prayer support as never before.

The divine commission still stands, "Go ye into all the world and preach the Gospel . . . and lo, I am with you alway." (Matthew 28: 20).

The command to go has not yet been revoked, and "the fields are white unto harvest, and the labourers are few". Our numbers of labourers on the Congo field are sadly depleted, there is more work than ever to do. The call still comes loud and clear as it did from Macedonia, Acts 16: 9 – "Come over . . . and help us."